Collaborative School Leadership

D0066594

Also available from Bloomsbury

Education in the Balance, Raphael Wilkins

Exploring the School Leadership Landscape, Peter Earley

Leading Schools in Challenging Circumstances, Philip Smith and Les Bell

Managing Staff for Improved Performance, David Middlewood and Ian Abbott

School and System Leadership, Sue Robinson

Sustainable School Transformation, edited by David Crossley

Collaborative School Leadership

Managing a Group of Schools

David Middlewood, Ian Abbott and Sue Robinson

Bloomsbury Academic
An imprint of Bloomsbury Publishing Plc

BLOOMSBURY
LONDON · OXFORD · NEW YORK · NEW DELHI · SYDNEY

Bloomsbury Academic

An imprint of Bloomsbury Publishing Plc

50 Bedford Square
London
WC1B 3DP
UK

1385 Broadway
New York
NY 10018
USA

www.bloomsbury.com

BLOOMSBURY and the Diana logo are trademarks of Bloomsbury Publishing Plc

First published 2018

© David Middlewood, Ian Abbott and Sue Robinson, 2018

David Middlewood, Ian Abbott and Sue Robinson have asserted their right under the
Copyright, Designs and Patents Act, 1988, to be identified as Authors of this work.

All rights reserved. No part of this publication may be reproduced or transmitted
in any form or by any means, electronic or mechanical, including photocopying,
recording, or any information storage or retrieval system, without prior
permission in writing from the publishers.

No responsibility for loss caused to any individual or organization acting on
or refraining from action as a result of the material in this publication can be
accepted by Bloomsbury or the authors.

British Library Cataloguing-in-Publication Data
A catalogue record for this book is available from the British Library.

ISBN: HB: 978-1-3500-0914-1
PB: 978-1-3500-0913-4
ePDF: 978-1-3500-0916-5
ePub: 978-1-3500-0915-8

Library of Congress Cataloging-in-Publication Data
A catalog record for this book is available from the Library of Congress.

Cover design by Terry Woodley
Cover image © enjoynz / Getty Images

Typeset by Newgen KnowledgeWorks Pvt. Ltd., Chennai, India
Printed and bound in Great Britain

To find out more about our authors and books visit www.bloomsbury.com.
Here you will find extracts, author interviews, details of forthcoming events
and the option to sign up for our newsletters.

Contents

Figures and Tables

Figures

Table

About the Authors

David Middlewood is currently a part-time Research Fellow at the Centre for Education Studies of the University of Warwick, UK, having previously worked at the Universities of Leicester and Lincoln. Prior to that, he worked in schools for many years and was headteacher of a comprehensive school for ten years. David has published twenty books on educational topics, many on human resources, and also on strategic management, extended schools, learning schools, practitioner research and professional learning. His various research projects have included ones on leadership teams, school support staff, appraisal, school cultures, succession planning, and raising achievement for disadvantaged children. He has taught and researched in countries as diverse as Greece, Seychelles, New Zealand and South Africa, and has been a visiting professor in the latter two countries. He was editor of two journals for school principals, primary and secondary, for six years. David has also been a research coordinator in a group of schools and has led enquiries and conferences on pupil and student voice.

Ian Abbott is Associate Professor and Director of the Centre for Education Studies at the University of Warwick, UK. Prior to higher education, he worked in schools and colleges in senior leadership roles for a number of years. He has worked in partnership with a number of external organizations, including Teach First and Teaching Leaders. He has collaborated with a number of schools and colleges on a range of research and staff development projects. He has significant international experience having worked in many countries, including Ethiopia, Tanzania, Brazil and China. His research interests include education policy and reform, school collaboration, utilization of the Pupil Premium, and initial teacher education. He has published widely on education policy and reform, teacher education and leadership, and staff development in schools and colleges.

Sue Robinson is Development Director of a charitable multi-academy trust specializing in primary academies. She was formerly an urban primary school headteacher, a national leader of education, and an associate of the National College for Teaching and Leadership. She gained her doctorate in 2012 and became a visiting fellow at University of Warwick, UK, in 2016. She has worked with many schools on leadership and professional development, with a special focus on system leadership and building leadership capacity. Her book on this was published in 2012.

David, Ian and Sue have collaborated on various topics relating to raising attainment for disadvantaged children. In addition, David and Ian have researched and taught together in the UK and abroad. They have co-authored a standard text on writing leadership dissertations; a book on improving professional learning through in-school enquiry in 2015, to which Sue contributed; and, most recently, one on managing staff performance (2017).

Abbreviations

ASCL	Association of School and College Leaders
CEO	chief executive officer
CMO	charter management organization
CPD	continuing professional development
CV	curriculum vitae
DCFS	Department for Children, Schools and Families
DfE	Department for Education
DFES	Department for Education and Science
EHT	Executive Headteacher
EMO	educational management organization
FGC	Family Group Conference
ISFS	independent state-funded school
LA	local authority
LLE	local leader of education
MAT	multi-academy trust
NASDC	New American Schools Development Corporation
NCSL	National College for School Leadership
NCTL	National College for Teaching and Leadership
NLE	national leader of education
NPM	new public management
NPQH	National Professional Qualification for Headship
OECD	Organisation for Economic Co-operation and Development
OFSTED	Office for Standards in Education
PISA	Programme for International Student Assessment
SLE	specialist leader of education
TSA	Teaching School Alliance
UK	United Kingdom
USA	United States of America
VC	voluntary-controlled

Preface

The origins of this book lie primarily in a number of research projects carried out in England by the three authors working together as a research team. These were commissioned projects, and together with a few other pieces of research done by two of the authors in the UK and certain African countries – some of which were commissioned and others were self-managed and self-motivated – the whole formed a considerable body of research data. The collected and analysed data gave, in our view, some valuable insights into one of the emerging and most widespread developments in the field of educational leadership at school level. This development is in the way schools are choosing – or being encouraged, incentivized or forced, depending on the political context – to work together to raise levels of attainment. This collaboration between schools and their leaders takes many different forms, depending on the context, whether that be regional or national. No doubt, many different forms of such collaboration between schools and leaders will continue to emerge in the coming years, but this book tries to draw together some of the implications of what has recently occurred and is currently taking place.

In examining the various forms that school collaboration can take in several countries, our focus has been on the implications of these on those in leadership roles in the schools, not on the actual nature of the forms of collaboration per se, although, of course, this affects the leadership and vice versa. Educational leadership is constantly evolving so that its effectiveness can meet the requirements of the time and perhaps anticipate the future demands of schools. Given that evidence from a number of countries points to a considerable shortage of personnel in education who have an ambition to become school leaders, the possibility that research into school leadership collaboration might prove useful was a further incentive.

The structure of the book reflects its research-based nature, with, in essence, the first part being context and theory; the second part the research itself; and the third part conclusions and implications. The three chapters of Part I begin with the description of the context of the educational landscape within which school leadership collaboration sits in Chapter 1. Chapter 2 covers the origins and general understanding of this collaboration in terms of what is known as system leadership, while Chapter 3 tries to describe the early origins of schools and their leaders working together and suggests some of the principles that seemed to underpin this kind of collaborative leadership.

Part II consists of five chapters that describe research carried out in five different forms of ways in which schools have been grouped or organized together, examining the implications of school leadership in each specific case. Chapter 4 investigates perhaps the simplest of these forms, where two school leaders work together to gain improvement for the schools – either for the supposed weaker school when it is paired with a successful one, or a state and fee-paying school for mutual benefit. Chapter 5 deals with the kind of leadership involved when schools are formed into groups known as federations (and these have developed into what are known as multi-academy trusts in England).

The academization of schools has been a major development in education in England and also in United States, and indeed, the whole issue of names and titles of groupings – and indeed of school leaders to some extent – is a complex and sometimes frustrating one in a book about the field of educational development where things change so rapidly. During the writing of this book, it is certainly true that new forms and titles continued to emerge! Chapters 6 and 7 deal with two separate kinds of groupings of schools, each of which involves its own specific kind of leadership. Chapter 6 covers the England model that involves a designated teaching school linked with a number of other schools that it supports in various ways and to various degrees. Chapter 7 examines the concept of schools/academies linked through a 'chain', a model found in England and the United States and a few other countries. A chain by its nature suggests a linear structure, and as examined in the chapters of Part II, different forms of school groupings have emerged, necessitating different kinds of leadership specific to a particular kind of grouping. What they have in common is that the school leaders concerned have to work collaboratively with various other people, including other leaders. The final chapter in Part II, Chapter 8, examines how school leaders, detached from their original school and often in an almost wholly strategic leadership role, manage their collaboration with the required personnel to ensure effectiveness across the group of schools. They are often known as 'executive leaders', although again, as the research indicates, a plethora of titles exists in such contexts.

Part III consists of three chapters that draw together some of the conclusions from the research and consider, speculate and discuss some of the implications arising from it. Chapter 9 attempts to make sense of the research in different contexts and offers insights into factors that may help identify key elements of effective collaborative leadership that itself may aid those involved in the future. Chapter 10 looks forward to a time, perhaps beyond the near future, when communities themselves, rather than the schools, will be central to collaboration. After all, collaboration in itself is a means to an end, as indeed is education. Finally, in Chapter 11, after reflecting on the implications of the new collaborative structures in education, especially schools, we briefly consider some of the implications and possible actions that may be needed in the immediate future to enable collaborative school leadership to improve and develop for the benefit of the learners in the schools and communities.

We are conscious that the majority of research carried out took place in England, but, as noted earlier, it also takes into consideration as many developments as possible in other countries. For example, Middlewood, Abbott, Netshandama and Whitehead (2017) write about different stages of collaboration development between schools and their leaders in South Africa and Tanzania, research that indicates part of the progress towards the reduction in school leaders' isolation through this development. For a variety of reasons described and discussed in this book, we believe this process is likely to continue, especially if we consider the urgent context of sustainability in education, where the isolation of individual schools and their leaders is perhaps not only undesirable but dangerous. Ultimately, the point of collaborating in effective practice is to raise the standard of learning and teaching and education as a whole to the level of the best schools. While good and excellent schools, no doubt, exist in virtually all countries, this is of only limited use to a nation if such schools operate in literally 'splendid' isolation, and perhaps jealously guarding their status. Only through working with other schools can overall standards be lifted, and as with all educational improvement, the role that school leaders play in this will remain central.

We owe a huge debt of gratitude to the many school leaders and other school staff who assisted us throughout this research and gave their time so generously to be interviewed. Thanks are due also to the various regional authority officers who commissioned some of the research and facilitated its implementation. We have changed their names to protect their identity, but the case examples in the book are real-life studies. We are grateful to Trish Caswell for her invaluable help in finalizing the manuscript and for the index. Thanks also go to Camilla Erskine and Maria Brauzzi at Bloomsbury for their help. Finally, David, Ian and Sue thank Jacqui, Deb and Graham, respectively, for their personal support in enabling the writing of this book.

David Middlewood, Ian Abbott and Sue Robinson
April 2017

Part One

A New Context for School Leadership

In the twenty-first century, school leadership and management continues to evolve and develop. One of the most striking developments is the way in which schools are learning – for a variety of reasons – to work with each other, collaborating in a number of areas. The first part of this book consists of three chapters that establish the background to this development. Chapter 1 sets out and examines the reasons why this movement has been growing, and, as one might expect, these are complex. Political pressure plays a large part as governments in many countries have become frustrated at the uneven progress in school improvement. The importance of school leadership is universally recognized if any improvement is required. Chapter 2 describes what is known as system leadership, whereby school leaders are seen as committing to the welfare and development of schools other than their own schools. This will ultimately lead to a self-improving system that relies much less on government policies and enables change to take place that is constant and embedded. This, of course, fits well with this century's concerns that leadership has to address issues of sustainability in its development, especially in schools with their concerns for future generations. Chapter 3 describes some of the very early attempts of school leaders working across more than a single school and discusses whether some principles can emerge from these initiatives which may prove to be relevant to those involved in twenty-first-century collaborative school leadership.

Chapter 1
From Isolation to Collaboration

Introduction

All education systems are under pressure to improve student performance and outcomes in an increasingly competitive world, which is experiencing rapid technological advances. Schools are at the forefront of these changes, and although in many countries the system as a whole is fragmenting, individual schools are increasingly being expected to collaborate with each other to enhance student performances and consequently produce better results. Collaboration between schools has been promoted by many central governments especially as the significance of the local authorities or districts diminishes. The focus on collaboration is becoming a world-wide issue and is seen by many as the basis for the only really effective way of developing sustainable school system improvement. This is set alongside a relentless drive to raise standards, often in a climate of diminishing resources. The relative isolation of schools as individual organizations is no longer either a possibility or a desirability.

In this chapter, we describe, discuss and explain the changing context in which school collaboration is being fostered and developed, the impact this has had on schools, and the significance of school leadership in this process. It therefore:

- considers the reasons why greater collaboration between schools is being encouraged by central governments;
- discusses the major policy initiatives designed to increase collaboration between schools;
- identifies the importance of effective leadership in securing school improvement through increased collaboration;
- explores the attempts to reduce inconsistency of achievements between schools by encouraging collaboration to reduce inequality.

Why is collaboration between schools being encouraged?

Fullan (1998: 2) describes that the fences of schools in countries such as Australia, Canada, the United States and the UK are 'tumbling down' as the realization came that education could not be seen as a panacea for all of societies' ills. In addition, according to Middlewood and Abbott (2015: 87), the other difficulties likely to be caused by schools and other public organizations operating in isolation include:

- research showing that there were a huge number of influences on effective learning, of which formal schooling was the only, albeit a very important, one;
- pressure on public services, including education, especially in increasingly pluralist, multi-ethnic societies;
- the realization that the huge sums of money expended on the disadvantaged ones were not paying dividends and there was a need to move the focus from remedial to preventative measures.

The lack of a coordinated and cooperative approach among various public services became increasingly clear, exposing a lack of clear accountability when problems occurred. Just as education is a part of a wider approach to sustainable development, so contact, communication and collaboration with the wider community and other schools is also essential. In countries like Australia, Canada, the United States and the UK – and those in Europe and Africa – developments since the 1990s have led to various forms of collaboration between schools, to the extent that many of these forms are promoted and even legislated by national governments. As Chapman (2015: 46) has argued,

> Interest in reforming leadership and governance arrangements to promote school-to-school collaboration has grown rapidly across several education systems. The United States, Sweden and England have continued to experiment with new approaches involving independent state-funded schools (ISFSs) such as a academies, charter schools and free schools and it has been argued these types of schools naturally lend themselves to the development of groups of schools working together as federations and chains under a single governance structure. (Policy Exchange, 2009)

The changes in school systems and the development of ISFSs have to be set in the context of broader changes that were taking place in the way public services were provided. In many countries, a market-led system underpinned by neo-liberalism has resulted in the creation of a so-called quasi-market in education (Le Grand and Bartlett, 1993). A quasi-market is similar to a free market, and competition is encouraged between providers (schools). At the same time, the state intervenes to ensure common approaches in areas such as assessment, curriculum and school inspection. Consumers – parents – are therefore encouraged to choose among schools, with information being provided to them through school inspection reports and league tables. According to Middlewood and Abbott (2015: 3), there is 'a system-wide move towards greater organisational autonomy which is taking place in many countries across the world, including some of the burgeoning economies such as China and India'. As schools take on increased roles and responsibilities, there has been a corresponding decline in the importance of the local authority or district. A system based broadly on some form of central control at either district or state level has been replaced by individual school autonomy within a framework controlled increasingly by national governments. This theme is developed in Chapter 2 when we consider, in particular, the diminishing role of the local authority. Education systems across the world have seen major changes in structure, organization and the way in which they operate, with schools being given greater freedom to develop links with a range of institutions. Hargreaves (2010) has proposed that this is a feature of a self-improving school system that would be structured around responses to local issues and school support, which in turn would lead to innovation and quality improvement.

So why has this been happening in so many countries over the last twenty years? Many national governments have moved towards a belief that the market knows best and that greater competition will lead to improved standards. Basically there has been a desire to raise the level of educational attainment as international comparisons grow in importance, for example, through international rankings such as the Organisation for Economic Cooperation and Development's (OECD) Programme for International Student Assessment (PISA). Almost every government is seeking to improve its relative position in international league tables. Increasing global competition and the perceived importance of an educated workforce to economic success have persuaded many countries to adopt a market-led approach to education provision. This has been apparent in developing and developed countries and has resulted in major reforms. This process has not been confined to education and can also be observed in other areas of the public sector, such as health, prisons and social care.

Owing to a decline in the authority of a central coordinating authority, a market-led approach can cause some problems in terms of overall provision of school places, effective planning and accountability. Increasingly schools will be working in isolation and there is a danger that there will not be any sharing of good practices, and mutual support will be diminished. Under any market-led system, schools that are successful will continue to grow, increasing student numbers and the possibility of new schools coming into operation. Conversely, schools that are less successful will lose student numbers and could eventually close down or be taken over by new providers (Ball, 2012). This opens up the possibility of one organization controlling a number of schools and should increase the likelihood of collaboration between schools, as all or several schools under the auspices of a single sponsor or governing authority seek to be managed in a relatively similar way.

Despite the threat of competition and potential pitfalls, there are a number of reasons why schools might still decide to work together:

- Education is still widely, if not universally, regarded as a human entitlement and therefore seen as predominantly part of a public or state provision. Within national education systems, there is still a focus on public service and a recognition that institutions should cooperate to benefit from the system as a whole;
- statutory regulations imposed by a funding agency which could be either central or local government;
- a realization that 'weaker' schools could benefit from the skills and expertise of more 'successful' schools;
- economies of scale enable improved service and greater choice;
- financial pressures;
- sharing of leadership skills and staff development opportunities;
- as a form of defensive reaction against perceived external threats;
- in some cases, schools may be compelled to work together because they are controlled by an external body, as noted above.

Different motives influence the capacity and desire of schools to work together. Individual staff have to be at the core of the process to facilitate any form of cooperation, and there has to be an expectation that some benefit will follow from the collaboration. A market-led system is likely to make it more difficult for schools to work together as self-interest and protection of their market position tend to predominate. In a system which is less market-oriented and less competitive, it should be easier to facilitate some form of collaboration. In reality, the situation is likely to be less clear cut, and there may be occasions when schools operating in a competitive market decide to work together, and schools that are part of a culture of cooperation decide against working together. A number of factors determine the extent of actual cooperation on the ground. External culture plays a significant part in determining levels of cooperation. Internally the culture of the school and the stance adopted by the headteacher or chief executive of a group of schools are likely to determine the opportunities for schools to work together. Within any school system that is perceived to be more or less successful, there is the likelihood that a form of collaboration can lead to dominant and subservient schools.

The type or extent of collaboration will also differ in different contexts and situations. At any given time, schools are likely to be involved in different levels of cooperation with other schools, which can change over time. It may be strategically advantageous to be involved at one point, but this may change in the future. External pressures will almost certainly change over time as education policy is constantly evolving. Barriers to cooperation among schools might be associated with time and resource constraints. Developing common approaches among schools will require a significant investment in staff time to ensure a consistent approach. In some cases, successful schools might not want to be associated with failing schools, at least not without considerable incentive or benefit to themselves. Within a competitive market, there is an inherent risk in cooperating with potential competitors, especially those deemed to be inferior in some way. At times there does appear to be a basic inconsistency in policy that encourages cooperation while fostering competition among schools in an attempt to improve standards.

At the heart of the policy lies a paradox between competition and collaboration. This is especially true when school funding is dependent on student numbers. It is in the self-interest of schools to compete with other schools for potential students because of the financial benefits from attracting additional student numbers. In a market-led system, staff recruitment and retention is another area where competition among schools is likely to occur. In England, for example, there are significant issues around teacher recruitment and retention; and in this case, schools are likely to remain highly competitive as they strive to recruit and retain the 'best' staff.

However, in practice, there will be different levels of cooperation among schools. Chapman (2015: 48–49) has identified a range of 'collaborative activity' based on a hierarchy of collaboration:

1. Association. This is a traditional model based on the involvement of a local authority or district to coordinate the process and is restricted to attendance at meetings and continuing professional development events.

2. Co-operation. A greater level of involvement which involves the opportunity to share current information and materials on a restricted basis.

3. Collaboration. This is based around the need to deal with specific issues and problems. It is commonly associated with a successful school supporting a school that is perceived to be failing and will involve shared knowledge and resources and restricted opportunities to create new information and materials.

4. Collegiality. A deeper and longer lasting relationship is developed which involves agreement around outcomes and approaches. Information is pooled and new material is developed to benefit all the partners.

(As chapters in Part II of this book describe the various models of collaboration that were investigated, it is interesting to consider the extent to which it is felt that they, or any of them, correspond to the categorization described by Chapman.)

As a consequence, several governments accept that some issues are better dealt with through collaboration both across schools and also with a range of other institutions. National policy initiatives such as No Child Left Behind in the United States and Every Child Matters in England and Wales are examples of this type of approach where all schools are obliged to collaborate to achieve particular outcomes.

Policy initiatives

Subsequent chapters of this book examine in more detail some of the specific policy initiatives that have been implemented to foster collaboration and their relationship to school leadership. In this section, we will consider broadly some of the more common types of collaboration. In England, a number of policies have been designed to foster school collaboration. The Beacon Schools initiative, London Challenge and the introduction of national leaders of education (NLEs) were early examples of policies designed to foster collaboration among schools.

The Beacon Schools initiative was intended to identify excellent schools (so-called Beacons) that would work with other schools to drive up standards, and were associated with wider government strategies to raise standards, especially in disadvantaged urban areas (Abbott, 2004; Abbott et al., 2013; Brown, 2015). The Beacon Schools received additional funding to share facilities, run training programmes and exchange staff. The long-term impact of this initiative appears to have been minimal, but it was one of the early examples of government policy designed to foster school collaboration in a system that was experiencing rapid fragmentation (Smith, 2015).England received support from the City Challenge initiative in a number of areas. Ainscow (2015) focusses on the Greater Manchester City Challenge initiative, and he describes how 'school-to-school partnerships of various kinds can help stimulate improvements in practice and expectations' (op cit: 2). The London Challenge was introduced as a response to the perceived failures of the schools across the city and was based around a system of successful headteachers providing support to those schools requiring improvement; see Barrs et al. (2014) and Hutchings et al. (2012). According to Muijs (2015: 565), 'working with other schools was considered a key factor in improving so-called "coasting" schools'. The support to bring about improvement of the schools in London was based around successful school leaders and teachers working with colleagues in schools that were deemed to be less successful. This approach was perceived to have more credibility than the employment of external consultants coming into schools to provide advice (Matthews and Hill, 2010).

The introduction of NLEs took this process a step further with the identification of successful headteachers across England who would have a remit to support underperforming schools. Muijis (2015) and the National College for Teaching and Leadership (NCTL, 2013a) have provided data that seem to suggest that this approach can be successful in improving outcomes in those schools receiving support.

Federations as a form of collaborative structure in England have grown in number and scope considerably since their introduction in the Education Act 2002, although there are some concerns about what the term 'federation' actually means (Chapman, 2015). According to the NCTL (2014: 1),

> The creation and membership of a federation is not just about structural change. It is also about a different mindset where the governors and school leaders share a commitment to improving the outcomes and life chances for all children across the federation, as opposed to just a single school, through a school-led system of raising standards and driving improvement.

While the ambiguity about the precise nature of what constitutes a federation continued and is discussed in Chapter 5, the use of the word 'mindset' here is a valuable insight into and indication of what might be seen as the key motivation for school collaboration. This is certainly true of professional motivation and, therefore, critical for the primary concern of this book – the nature of the school leadership for effective collaboration.

More specifically, according to NCTL (2014: 4), schools decide to federate to:

- address or prevent school failure;
- ensure viability and achieve economies of scale; and
- create more integrated provision across phases.

In England, groups of academy schools controlled by a multi-academy trust (MAT) have become the main form of school collaboration. The situation surrounding the various types of school organization has become complicated with a wide range of different types of school. We return to some specific school examples to illustrate key concepts later in the book, and it will be useful here to briefly explain the different types of school structure. Therefore, we will define some terms that will aid understanding.

Maintained schools

These are under the control of the local authority or district, and they are required to follow the national curriculum and national terms of staff pay and conditions. To complicate matters further, there are four main types of maintained schools:

- Community schools are under the full control of the local authority through the school's governing body.
- Foundation or trust schools are owned and operated by the governing body or a charitable trust.

- Voluntary-aided (VA) schools have been set up by a voluntary body (often a church board) but are financed by the local authority. The governing body employs the staff and has control over student admissions.
- Voluntary-controlled (VC) schools are funded and run by the local authority. The local authority sets admissions policies and employs the staff.

Academies

These schools are funded by the state but are independent of the local authority or district. They have a legally binding funding agreement with the Department of Education. They have greater control over curriculum and pay and conditions for staff. Schools can become academies through three routes:

- Sponsored academies were designated as underperforming schools that were removed from local authority control. The sponsors could be charitable foundations, other schools, individuals and faith groups. The role of the sponsor is to facilitate school improvement, although early sponsored academies received financial support from their sponsor.
- Convertor academies are schools, according to DfE, that are performing at a sufficiently high level to choose to become an academy and opt out of local authority control.
- Free schools are the only way in which new schools can be opened, and they are automatically new academies. Groups such as parents, teachers, charities, universities community and faith groups can all apply to establish a free school.

Academies can operate as individual institutions, but, increasingly, chains of academies known as MATs have been established. A MAT is made up of a number of individual schools, but there is one organization that actually runs the schools. Schools within a MAT lose their individual legal identity and are responsible to the trust. The MAT enters into a legally binding agreement with the DfE to run the schools within the trust. Many MATs are run by successful schools that take poor performing schools into academy chains; see, for example, Hill et al. (2012). Some of the leadership and school improvement issues that can arise from MATs are considered in Chapter 5. Salokangas and Chapman (2014: 383), in their study of two academy chains, claim that 'a system is being created through which sponsors, rather than individual academies, hold significant decision-making competence, which may or may not permit academy-level autonomy'.

Another strand of policy that aims to foster collaboration between schools is the teaching schools initiative. Teaching schools were established in 2010 and are schools recognized as 'outstanding', providing a range of support and training opportunities to other schools and their staff. The creation of a teaching school alliance is voluntary, and the focus of their work is on six key areas:

- initial teacher training
- school-to-school support
- continued professional development
- research and development
- specialist leaders of education
- succession planning and talent management.

Case example 1A gives the perspective of one school leader of such a collaborative group.

Case example 1A

Anna is the headteacher of a large teaching school in the north of England. The school has a track record of working with other schools and was designated a teaching school in 2011. According to Anna,

> Working with other schools is something we are committed to do, in a variety of ways. It is not because we think we are better than others, or out to tell others what to do; it is because we are successful and want to share that success with other schools; it's about establishing trust and a genuine professional partnership. We want to help improve the system as a whole and to support other schools and teachers to reach the same standards and levels that we have. I am not so arrogant that I think we know it all. We are always learning from other schools that we work with, even when their levels are not as officially as good as ours. I know we cannot change the whole system but by working together we can at least help some of the schools and most importantly help the students as well. All of us do have a responsibility for the whole system. I didn't come into teaching just for me or my school. It is important that you do have a wider perspective of the situation.

In Chapter 6, we look at the work of teaching schools in more detail, as we consider the leadership involved. However, in terms of preparation for leadership, the NCTL (2015: 10) gives an outline of the support available to staff in a teaching school alliance:

> The alliance also supports the progression of staff to headship through delivery of National Professional Qualifications for Headship (NPQH), offering secondments and exchanges between partner schools to broaden and deepen learning of school contexts that an emerging headteacher may not have yet acquired. The alliance also now offers progression routes to becoming an Executive Leader and setting up a multi academy trust through a programme of one to one support, governor support and capacity building seminars.

Currently, there are over 600 teaching schools working in alliances with over 7,000 schools (Greany, 2016). According to an evaluation of the project, the teaching schools initiative appears to be working well while recognizing the pressures of schools having to maintain their own success (Gu et al., 2015).

Such collaborative structures can also be found in a number of other countries such as The Netherlands, where schools that are part of a federation are led and managed by principals. These principals may lead one or more schools within a particular federation, which may in addition include the post of 'superintendent', who is an educational professional responsible for operational management (Collins et al., 2005). In Norway, some schools combine as one unit for administration that is governed by one principal (Higham et al., 2009) In Flanders, school federations are organized regionally, and joining one is voluntary. Piot and Kelchermans (2016) note that one reason schools are 'stimulated' to join is by the provision of extra financial resources. According to Muijs (2015: 564), 'In the USA we have seen the emergence of Charter Management Organisations running networks of Charter schools and many other school networks (such as the League of Professional Schools) exist.'

Sometimes the actual form of the collaborative structure is less important than the fact that it happens at all! Certainly, it can, at the very least, reduce the isolation of the school, especially of the principal, as Case example 1B makes clear.

Case example 1B

William is the principal of a large secondary school in a rural part of Tanzania. The school is popular but has limited resources and faces a number of challenges, including student drop-out, teacher absenteeism, staff recruitment pressures and restricted opportunities for staff professional development. William commented,

> On a personal level, it's good to cooperate with others to share problems and talk about issues. Being a principal can be a lonely job, especially when your school is such an isolated one as ours is. We try to work closely with our primary schools; our facilities are not great but they are so much better than theirs. It's good to see what can be achieved with a bit of mutual cooperation. Collaboration around common issues with other secondary schools is also becoming increasingly important. After all, it is really all about our students and young people as a whole. We are only at an early stage (of collaboration) but we are able to learn from each other and hopefully this will help towards making the system better as a whole. It is so easy to become isolated and blame others, but we do have a professional duty to work together with others to improve what is going on overall.

Leadership

The major structural changes that have been taking place with the decline of local authorities, the growth of autonomous schools and the development of a quasi-market have been described. These changes have coincided with the growth of New Public Management (NPM) (Hall, 2013). McLaughlin et al. (2002) identified NPM as the 'dominant paradigm' in the UK, parts of Scandinavia, Australia and the United States. Middlewood and Abbott (2017a: 7) argue that 'NPM is a reflection of the reform of the public education system which embodies privatisation, increased choice, performance management, use of private sector management approaches and greater accountability'. They go on to argue that NPM impacts on staff by ensuring:

- a focus on increased competition throughout the education system;
- a greater focus on target setting for individuals and organizations;
- additional emphasis on measurable outcomes with increased surveillance of individual performance;
- greater scrutiny of financial performance with a focus on value for money;
- funding being related to student numbers; and
- diversification of income streams.

(Middlewood and Abbott, 2017a: 7)

There is a tendency for schools operating with these pressures to adopt a more managerialist approach and to reduce the opportunities for teacher autonomy within a self-improving system. Schools may decide that they are faced with no alternative but to look inwards. The danger with this approach is that schools concentrate solely on their own performance at the expense of others in the system. A potential way to overcome the tendency of schools to respond to these pressures by becoming insular is to encourage schools to cooperate. In England, according to Greany (2014), there are four principles that underpin the government's approach to such a system that ultimately would become a self-improving system:

- Teachers and schools are responsible for their own improvement.
- Teachers and schools learn from each other and from research so that good practice spreads.
- The best schools and leaders extend their reach across other schools so that all schools improve.
- Government support and intervention is minimized.

With a decline in direct central and local government involvement, headteachers have been given a key role to play in a self-improving school system. Governments in a number of countries have sought to increase individual headteachers' autonomy, and they have been encouraged to develop system leadership. Leithwood et al. (2006: 5) have argued that 'there is not a single documented case of a school successfully turning around its pupil achievement trajectory in the absence of talented leadership'. A key element of the developing role of some headteachers in England is the creation of executive headteachers (EHT). An EHT is a person who 'directly leads two or more schools in a federation or other partnership arrangement' (DfE, 2015). According to Lord et al. (2016: 3), 'Executive headteachers often work to oversee the transition and improvement of schools; as well as grow partnerships between schools.'

We examine in more detail the key roles played by headteachers and principals in developing collaboration through school-to-school support, in a variety of forms, in Chapters 4–7 – and more specifically EHT's role in Chapter 8. Given the central role played by the headteacher or principal in determining the success of an individual school, it is clear that this impact could be spread to other schools as part of a self-improving system.

It would clearly be illogical if good practice developed in one school was not made available to other parts of the system. However, unless there are specific polices in place to enable this process to take place, a fragmented system operating under the constraints of a quasi-market can discourage sharing of good practice because of the competitive nature of the system. Hanushek et al. (2013: 228) have argued that there are significant differences in the impact of school autonomy on raising student achievement levels between developed and developing countries:

> Does school autonomy make sense everywhere? Our results suggest the answer is a clear 'no': The impact of school autonomy on student achievement is highly heterogeneous, varying by the level of development of a country. The overall result may have broader implications for the generalizability of findings across countries and education systems. It suggests that lessons from educational policies in developed countries may not translate directly into advice for developing countries, and vice versa.

At the same time as the importance of the headteacher or principal in bringing about school improvement has increased, many school systems have seen the growth of distributed leadership. In many countries, there has been a subtle movement away from sole emphasis on the importance of individual school leaders towards recognition of the greater significance of teams, and the establishment of networks of schools, their leaders and staff. There has been a growing acceptance that the leadership skills necessary to run a complicated organization such as a school cannot be restricted to one person or indeed to those in formal leadership positions (Diamond and Spillane, 2016; Harris, 2013). Distributed leadership draws on the expertise of a number of staff within an organization and does not limit participation to a small group of senior managers. While there has been widespread acceptance and implementation of distributed leadership, especially among practitioners, there is still some debate about the effectiveness and impact of distributed leadership (see, e.g. Gronn, 2016; Lumby, 2016). Despite distributed leadership remaining a contested topic, it continues to grow in importance 'as an important framework for thinking about educational practice' (Diamond and Spillaine, 2016: 152). A number of countries, including Saudi Arabia and Qatar, are undertaking significant investment in distributed leadership in the belief that it will lead to school improvement and higher standards. Distributed leadership is referred to in various places in later chapters as part of the ways in which school leadership is affected by collaboration with other schools, especially where headteachers or principals are required to be out of schools for greater periods of time.

Reducing inequality

One of the main drivers of education policy has been attempts to bring about about improvement in both individual schools and the whole schooling system. There has been a drive to raise overall standards as well as a desire by policymakers to reduce inequalities and close the gap between students from affluent backgrounds and their counterparts who are more disadvantaged. In both developed and developing countries, a major problem has been inconsistency of achievement – the gap between the best and worst of schools. The realization by policymakers that there is little point in having a few outstanding schools where others are weak has encouraged collaboration between schools as a serious attempt to reduce inequalities.

As a starting point, a significant number of school collaboration initiatives, as outlined earlier in the chapter, were designed to achieve system-wide improvement. However, in practice, many of the initiatives are based on one successful school working with, taking over or providing support to one or more less successful schools. Supporting these less successful schools is seen as inevitably resulting in raising levels of student achievement and hopefully reducing inequalities between groups of students. However, there has been growing criticism of top-down policy approaches, and this approach has been described as 'increasingly inadequate' and 'notoriously impotent to change behaviour in teaching and learning' (OECD, 2015). A system that promotes collaboration between institutions and allows staff to learn from each other may have a better chance of being successful at reducing inequality. At the very least, it will allow some degree of flexibility into the system and enable the local context to be taken into consideration. Within a broad policy framework, collaborative initiatives, such as the teaching schools in England and Wales, may allow opportunities for a recognition that local conditions and circumstances can be significant factors in determining inequality of provision and outcome. Any approaches to reduce that inequality, therefore, need to take account of such factors.

It is worth noting early in this book that, while political and economic issues are explored in research so far into collaborative processes in education, little is known to date about the impact if any on the communities that the schools or groups of schools serve; and while accountability at national levels is discussed, accountability to stakeholders such as parents is relatively unexplored. This, of course, may be because of the early stage that collaboration between schools is perceived to be.

Conclusion

We have outlined a number of factors that have contributed to the growth of school-to-school collaboration. We have also introduced a number of specific policy initiatives that have been introduced to encourage and enable such collaboration to take place. It is difficult to disagree with Middlewood et al. (2017: 164) who claim that 'various models of collaborative practice exist but what all the most effective ones have in common is the capacity for those involved to learn from each other'. However, as Muijs (2015: 565–6) has rightly pointed out, 'As with any other school improvement intervention, collaboration is unlikely to be a panacea for improvement, and conditions and strategies will need to be in place for it to be successful.' A variety of such models where research was undertaken by the book's authors are described in later chapters, with an emphasis on the leadership involved as well as their conditions and strategies for success. In the next chapter, the focus is on examining the aspects of system leadership.

Summary

This chapter has:

- explored the policy reasons why greater collaboration between schools has been promoted by central government, especially in England;
- stressed on some of the major school collaboration polices that have been introduced;
- described the significance of effective leadership in bringing about school improvement as part of greater school collaboration; and
- identified the significance of policies designed to reduce inequality.

Recommended reading

Ainscow, M. (2015). *Towards self-improving school systems: Lessons from a city challenge*. Abingdon: Routledge.

Desforges, C. (2006). *Collaboration for transformation: Why bother?* Nottingham: National College for School Leadership.

Middlewood, D., Abbott, I., Netshandama, V., and Whitehead, P. (2017). Policy leadership, school improvement and staff development in England, Tanzania and South Africa: Schools working together. In P. Miller (ed.), *Cultures of educational leadership*. London: Palgrave Macmillan.

Chapter 2
System Leadership

Introduction

In developed countries across the world, there is a need to find solutions to educate an increasingly knowledge-based economy with fast-moving technological changes (Higham et al., 2009; Spring, 2008). This is also linked to a perceived need to improve performance in schools and a dearth of school leaders wishing to undertake leadership roles (Pont, 2008b). The success of borrowing policy in education may depend not just on context but also on the stage of development of an individual nation's school system. Mourshed et al. (2010: 3) identified a 'consistent cluster of interventions', which were different from each other but which characterized school systems in different countries on a continuum of performance.

Possible solutions have led to calls in varying degrees in countries such as England, Finland, Canada and Australia to develop the role of school leaders to lead the education system. This use of school leaders has in turn led to a requirement for greater autonomy for those leaders to have the freedom to lead. Greater autonomy has also been accompanied by greater accountability in England, which has sought to be 'intelligent' (Hopkins, 2006) in its use of mechanisms to hold school leaders accountable.

This chapter therefore

- considers what were the background contextual issues leading to calls for change and which policies were implemented to deal with them;
- examines why a 'critical mass' (Fullan, 2004) of school leaders was deemed necessary to effect change;
- describes how this changed their roles and developed new roles;
- explores the leadership styles and characteristics appropriate to system leadership; and
- considers how capacity is developed and improvement sustained.

Background and rationale for the development of system leadership

What is a system?

Systems leadership or leadership across multiple organizations or systems is not a concept limited to education but can be found in other sectors such as business and other public sectors, including the National Health Service in the UK (Welford et al., 2012). This chapter is concerned with the leadership of one particular system – education, and specifically that of schools. It is not intended to offer a detailed perspective on organizational theory, but it is useful to consider why the use of systems leadership has entered the realm of school improvement.

Its roots lie in 'systems thinking' and particularly the work of Senge (1990: 44) who referred to a system as 'the key relationships that influence behaviour over time'. Kofman and Senge (1995: 27) argued that a system 'cannot be understood as a function of its isolated components' and what each of them is doing, but should be considered in terms of 'how each part is interacting with the rest'.

Welbourn et al. (2012: 10), while acknowledging the simplicity of their definition, note the differences between an organization and a system. An organization can be loosely defined as an independent, self-contained and separate entity. A system comprises a series of connected, interrelated and interacting parts where the decisions and actions of one part or entity have consequences for the others in the system.

Is a single school an organization – that is, a self-contained, separate entity; or is it a system of connected interrelated parts? Collarbone and West-Burnham (2007: 13) suggest that 'schools are systems within systems', because schools are interdependent and can be understood as an interacting set of relationships. Educational schools' systems are highly complex and comprise many interconnected parts in the form of schools as both singular and multiple institutions. Depending on their structure, governance and possibly inclination, schools can also form interdependent relationships with agencies such as sponsors, dioceses and local authorities (LAs).

Managing change in a system

Introducing change into the education system is a 'complex adaptive challenge' (Heifetz, 1994) because simple technical solutions are unsuitable to manage change due to the complexity of the system. Instead of a single solution to a single problem, successful system change entails thinking about whole and interrelated systems. It is not appropriate to reduce 'complex problems into separate rationally managed components' (Hargreaves, 2003: 71).

The complexity in the system also makes change difficult to predict or control, and there are often unintended consequences. Chapman (2002: 20) refers to difficulties in predicting the consequences of policy because of the 'non-linear' interactions among the components of the system. Therefore, a 'cyclical process' where 'the impact of change' is considered in relation to the whole system and its relationships (NSBA, n.d.) is necessary This lessens the likelihood of tensions in policy, for example, among the competing interests of stakeholders.

An additional complication is that organizations can be slow to adapt to change (March and Olsen, 1989). Educational policy often tends to have short-term solutions to meet short-term goals such as measurement of test results or performance league tables. In England, there has not been time for the school system to adapt gradually to the constant turbulent change imposed by successive governments, which has also contributed to the contradictory tensions described earlier and, to use Clarke and Newman's (1997) term, an increasingly 'fragmented policy domain'.

Direct intervention, or centrally imposed policy reform that controls what happens, is considered by Bentley (2002) as being unsuitable for the complexities of the situation because this sort of system tends to control the actions and values of people. Instead, it is argued that what is needed for strategies for reform to be successful is the 'active consent' (Hargreaves, 2003: 72) or engagement of 'the idealism and commitments' (Levin, 2012) of those involved.

As a response to the difficulty of predicting change and to managing systemic challenges, there have been calls for leadership of the system from within, that is, from successful school leaders who implement educational reforms (Fullan, 2004; Hargreaves, 2010–12) and who may be better equipped to solve the issues as they arise.

Successful system change in education is about shifting from single leaders and schools to system leaders working between and across multiple organizations, as examined later in this chapter.

Calls for change

The policy landscape within which system leadership operates was detailed in Chapter 1. It is, however, worth outlining here what were the issues that system leadership was meant to address and why it was advocated as a policy response.

Policy context 2002–10

During this period in England, there was recognition by policy advisers, including the Chief Adviser on Schools Standards (2002–2005), of the need to address two issues. These were a perceived plateauing of standards and a dearth of applicants for school leadership roles to replace the retirement of the so-called 'baby boomer' generation of school staff (Hopkins, 2006).

Certain policies drove key areas of change in education, which included workforce reform (DfE, 2003) and changes to the curriculum and testing aimed at raising standards (DfES, 2004). In addition, changes were made to the Ofsted schools' inspection framework as part of a drive for 'intelligent accountability' (Hopkins, 2006) to make inspection more responsive to school performance. Social justice was also used as a driver for improvement through the Every Child Matters agenda (DCSF, 2009). Changing patterns of school leadership developed to include new roles for school leaders as recognition grew that the top-down imposition of policy was ineffective.

In the context of the development of system leadership in England, it is important to note that these policies were introduced partly due to a recognition that a micro-management approach was no longer suitable to effect whole-system school improvement. A government could not control the effects of its policies. Managerialism had become a dominant thread running through the schools system via its call for the setting of performance targets and the measurement of these as part of the government's accountability systems most notably through the inspection service, Ofsted. While setting tests and monitoring performance was common to many countries, including Canada, Australia, the United States and New Zealand, the use of an inspection regime such as Ofsted was not. There are, however, mechanisms to measure performance across countries in international tables such as the use of Progress in International Reading Literacy Studies; Trends in Mathematics and Science Study; and the Programme for International Students Assessment.

The effect of managerialism on the role of school leaders in England was the creation of a type of leadership constrained by the increased level of bureaucracy that resulted in managing and implementing government policies. Collarbone and West-Burnham (2008: 15) refer to a command-and-control approach from top-down government policies that created a form of dependency culture in schools, resulting in 'a loss of confidence and lack of initiative' from school leaders. Managing the role of school leaders in this way had, therefore, produced a form of compliance leading to the identification of what Gronn (2003) termed 'designer leadership'. Instead, leadership needed to be encouraged that could respond effectively to complex and rapid change (Bentley, 2003). Consequently, a new approach to the implementation of policy by schools was adopted, which 'necessitated changes to the role of headteacher' and 'the creation of new patterns of school leadership' (Robinson, 2012: 20).

Policy context 2010–15

While some improvement had been made to standards and performance by 2010, standards in schools had plateaued and early improvements had not been sustained. Succession management was also an ongoing issue for the reason referred to earlier. A white paper on 'The Importance of Teaching' (2010) represented a fundamental philosophical shift in policy (see Chapter 1). It heralded organizational change in the form of greater diversity of school structures and greater autonomy for schools and school leaders, combined with a rigorous accountability system. The aims were to increase parental choice and to raise academic standards through extending the system leadership of accredited headteachers and senior leaders, validated by Ofsted as 'outstanding'.

The freedom to innovate was introduced by the Labour government and implemented through the Innovations Unit. This concept was extended by the UK Coalition government to include freedom to open a free school, a converter academy, or by collaborating through an extension of academy chains, multi-academy trusts (MATs) and federations (DfE, 2010). The government was influenced by what it perceived as the success of the Charter movement in the United States. Some charter schools have moved in the recent past from a single-school approach to one that used a network of schools with 'central office support' (Farrell et al., 2012).

In addition to structural reform, a new key element of policy was to use the 'best' school leaders to drive its reforms in what Hargreaves (2010) termed a self-improving school system. With the acknowledgement that the top-down command-and-control approach had not worked, a policy of encouraging outstanding school leaders to become system leaders –enabled through a combination of high autonomy linked to high accountability – was signalled:

> collaboration in the future will be driven by school leaders and teachers – not bureaucrats. (DfE, 2010: 52)

Policy context since 2015

The white paper (2016a: 13) stated its intentions to continue to use the 'best' school leaders and to 'extend their reach' to drive reform, and it noted that a system with greater autonomy had greater dependence on 'outstanding educational leaders' (ibid: 13). Despite advocating a self-improving system and seeking to ensure an appropriate environment for system leadership to flourish, challenges continued to emerge. Policy and structural changes introduced greater complexity into the system. The educational system became more fragmented, making the use of a whole-system approach more complicated or challenging. In addition, school budgets and other resources available to schools were reduced; the shortage of school leaders continued and the birth rate began to rise, exacerbating the need for more schools and school leaders. The need to find solutions became an imperative.

Using school leaders as agents of change: the development of system leadership

Most headteachers in England have always been involved in some form of collaboration or networking (Hill, 2006), but these are identified as increasingly important for effective school improvement (Chapman et al., 2010). What represented a systemic change in England in the early years of the twenty-first century was the combination of 'central initiatives' and the agency of headteachers (Higham et al., 2009). The policy discourse of government and policy advisers (Fullan, 2004; Hargreaves, 2003, 2010–12; Hopkins, 2006) highlighted the importance of participants having a role in transforming the system and solving systemic issues of underperformance.

Fullan (2004) described effecting a whole-system change through the use of leadership practice as 'system thinkers in action' who actively participate in 'linking to other parts of the system'. He argued that effective whole-system reform depended on getting a 'critical mass' of leaders with the characteristics and sense of moral purpose to lead across the system by supporting the improvement of other local schools. Hopkins and Higham (2007: 148) argue that it is the 'substantive engagement' of heads, 'willing to shoulder wider system roles' in leading across schools, that distinguishes system leadership from other forms of collaboration. It was expected that school leaders would not only improve the attainment and progress of children in other local schools but also be accountable for it (Hill, 2011).

This clearly involved school leaders working together, and such practice has begun to develop with greater interdependence among leadership teams in Belgium, Finland and England, although not when it is compulsory. In Finland, for example, collaboration is not 'contrived' but formed as part of a culture of trust and cooperation, which encourages 'risk taking' and innovation (Hargreaves et al., 2008: 85).

Autonomy and accountability

One of the difficulties in developing a 'critical mass' of school leaders in England in the early years of the twenty-first century was the influence of managerialism as previously described. The level of prescription and micro-management led to a low level of autonomy for headteachers. The UK government perceived that it needed to offer a degree of autonomy to school leaders to implement the reforms without a prescribed process of 'how to do it' at school level. These school leaders needed to be trusted, and so it was important that they 'earned' autonomy (Morris, 2001). By 2010, the importance of autonomy for outstanding school leaders had been established, and the white paper (DfE, 2010) claimed that the 'benefits of school autonomy had been established beyond doubt' (ibid: 11).

If school leaders were to support other schools, they had to have the required skills and credibility to be considered effective. Any autonomy of leadership earned by them should be gained through a fair process. Usually in England, this was the result of validation from an 'outstanding' leadership judgement from Ofsted, pivotal to the success of which was the high performance of pupils in standardized tests. Inspection can have unintended consequences in that schools will 'play the game' and do what they think is necessary to secure a good inspection and play safe rather than take innovative risks and face potential failure (Robinson, 2012). In addition, there is no guarantee that because a school is successful in tests, the leader will necessarily be able to replicate success elsewhere. Greany (2014) argues that Ofsted may have become 'too dominant as a force for change' and has led to 'unhealthy friction' between Ofsted and the school leaders who are leading improvement in their schools.

English school leaders have been recognized as being among the most autonomous across the world with some evidence that balancing high autonomy with high accountability is a feature common to several high-performing countries (Greany, 2015a). In addition to using inspection as a way for school leaders to earn autonomy, legislation was enacted to create the opportunity for schools to convert to academy status and thereby be free from the perceived constraints of being schools maintained by LAs. There is some evidence from a DfE report (Cirin, 2014) that academies have used the increased autonomy gained from legislation and further increased their freedom to make decisions about their schools, for example, by changing their curriculum, linking pay to performance, and using wider procurement services.

Need for leaders to collaborate

While acknowledging the variety in formality of partnerships, Hargreaves (2010) advocated 'deep partnerships' and different types of 'families' or clusters of schools, led by suitably interested and skilled leaders who would promote school improvement through shared leadership knowledge and practice. These collaborations could achieve what single schools cannot, that is, 'innovation, knowledge transfer, economies of scale and sharing capacity'. Higham et al. (2009) noted that system leaders in collaboration and partnership take 'greater joint responsibility' for the outcomes for a wider group of pupils in a community. There are some international comparisons for collaboration across schools. Farrell et al. (2012) observe that the Charter organizational model in the United States offers this form of collaboration to combat the challenges faced by 'stand-alone' charter schools and to achieve economies of scale.

Diminishing role of the local authority

Successive government policies led to a diminishing level of influence, control and mediating force of the LAs (see Chapter 1). As well as having a reduction in funding, they were increasingly less able to offer support for school improvement, and there has been a loss of 'local intelligence' deemed essential to broker system leadership (Higham et al., 2009). Brokering the roles of school leaders led to some LAs taking on a linking role as part of their response to their statutory responsibility for failing schools (Abbott et al., 2013). Simkins (2015) found that LAs were endeavouring to enhance collaboration in their localities but also recognized that the choice to participate was in the hands of the schools themselves. Some headteachers view LAs as a 'stumbling block' for effective partnership due to their lack of support for schools to change status or expand their role as executive heads to work in other local schools (NCSL, 2013). Case example 2A illustrates how an LA officer in 2016 sought to work with headteachers to provide system leadership for vulnerable schools with limited success.

Case example 2A

Elizabeth is a senior officer in a LA located in a shire county in the English Midlands. She has a very good understanding of the aims of system leadership, having been involved with the National College and the DfE. While Elizabeth was committed to a self-improving system led by schools, she felt that it was an initiative that was not yet mature enough to cope without an 'infrastructure' or 'safety net' provided by the LAs. Her challenge was to create an approach that would use successful school leaders to support vulnerable schools but within a climate where she only could persuade and influence headteachers without the power to direct their work.

Before undertaking her current role, Elizabeth already had considerable experience from another LA of working with and deploying system leaders successfully. She hoped to use her knowledge of the barriers and opportunities associated with this work.

One of the major differences she encountered in her current role was the nature of the challenge. Most of the schools felt they had no major issues, and there were only some pockets of deprivation, which contrasted with the 'massive deprivational challenges' previously met. Elizabeth believed that lack of challenge led to a complacency that did not breed creativity. Building relationships is key. Elizabeth met heads to discover their views and experience of system leadership and to set out her own vision. She quickly learned who would be supportive, where capacity was, and where the potential for capacity existed.

Early meetings with NLEs, heads of teaching schools and other leaders of outstanding schools were used to set the scene and gauge interest in a system leadership. Elizabeth acknowledges in using this small group she was 'preaching to the converted' but 'it was a start'. Over the course of several months of meetings, the group decided that it would create a countywide challenge board with the aim of identifying, challenging and offering support to vulnerable schools. The board would be robust, with clear accountability measures built into it. Membership would comprise headteachers, the regional schools commissioner and Ofsted, and Elizabeth would represent the LA to support them.

Support would be short-term, and Elizabeth argued for a sense of urgency to ensure a sustainable school improvement. The consultation for the national funding formula made it clear that the public services grant would be reduced or eliminated. As this grant pays for the school improvement service, the consequences of its withdrawal would be that Elizabeth will no longer be able to support school leaders in their work with vulnerable schools.

Calls for system redesign were predicated on recognition of the 'centrality' of headship in English schools (Southworth, 2008) and, therefore, the importance of the role of the headteacher in leading and delivering the reforms in schools. The next section examines the new roles that were developed to promote system leadership and the context in which they were and are used.

The success of the challenge board in the case example was because of the drive and commitment of Elizabeth and some headteachers who wanted to support schools across the LA. It remains to be seen if it is sustainable if the initiators among the heads and LA move on.

Roles undertaken by school leaders engaged in system leadership

The roles undertaken by school leaders in different countries have become more complex in the last ten years. Examples include Finland (Pont et al., 2008a) and Hong Kong, or regions such as Shanghai (Jensen and Clark, 2013) or the Charter movement in the United States (Farrell et al., 2012). Traditionally, headteachers in the UK led a single institution, and while they may have worked collaboratively, the role of headteacher was recognized as leading one school. As a response to the need for reform described earlier, system leadership became an umbrella term for the many varied and interconnected roles beginning to be undertaken by school leaders. Higham et al. (2009) suggest it is the leadership practised through these roles that makes their holders system leaders rather than the name of the role. Greany (2015b) noted, prior to the focus on system leadership, that the government's response to school improvement had been to retain effective school leaders in their own schools and concentrate on leadership development programmes or 'fresh starts' to support leaders and schools. Gunter (2012) suggests these initiatives were a mechanism to rectify failure rather than a positive move. It was considered to be more effective to improve schools by relying on the first-hand leadership expertise of effective headteachers rather than external consultants (Hill and Matthews, 2008). Consequently, there was a growth in the use and type of system leadership roles, some of which were 'nationally mandated' and others developed locally (Higham et al., 2009: 12). A brief overview of some of the important roles for school leaders from a national, middle-tier and local partnerships perspective is given.

National roles

The determining characteristic of national roles is the formality and provision of guidelines and accountability associated with them.

National leaders of education

In 2005, the National College for School Leadership (NCSL) was asked to identify a group of most 'effective heads' drawn from schools in the most challenging circumstances as national leaders of education (NLEs; DfES, 2005). The role was then introduced in 2006 with the designation initially of sixty-eight headteachers (Hill and Matthews, 2008) who had at least three years of experience in a school designated by Ofsted as outstanding and proven experience of supporting other schools. By 2016, there were 1,100 NLEs. Their roles were to

- support schools in challenging and vulnerable circumstances,
- advise government on education policy, and
- advise NCSL on the leadership development of future leaders of education (NCSL, 2007: 4).

In addition to the designation of the headteacher as NLE, the outstanding school they led became designated as a National Support School with the expectation that other leaders in the school would also offer school-to-school support.

There are parallels elsewhere, and Jensen and Clark (2013) describe the empowered management programme in Shanghai with the aim of reducing inequality between schools as having 'strong similarities' with the NLE programme; it uses successful school leaders to support low-performing schools for an extended period of two to five years.

Local leaders of education

Introduced in 2008, local leaders of education (LLEs) complemented the role of NLEs. While there was some blurring of the roles in reality, it was not expected that LLEs would also use their schools as supporting schools. The criteria were similar in that the headteacher needed to have been judged as outstanding, but the role differed in that they were expected to 'coach or mentor new headteachers or headteachers whose schools are in challenging circumstances'. In 2016, the functions of an LLE were to work in schools where:

- attainment is below the minimum standards set out by the government;
- the school is considered to be at risk of not achieving the minimum standards of attainment or going into special measures; and
- a new, first-time headteacher has been appointed.

(www.gov.uk/guidance/system-leaders-who-they-are-and-what-they-do)

Specialist leaders of education

There was recognition by government and generated through the NCSL's designation of specialist leaders of education (SLEs) that even if a school was not deemed outstanding overall, there were nevertheless areas of outstanding practice in these schools from middle or senior leaders. If these could be judged, validated and deployed (often temporarily for specific projects), these would be an added resource for school improvement and wider system leadership. By 2016, the National College for Teaching and Leadership (NCTL) noted that these areas covered 'the four focus areas of inspection', namely leadership and management, pupil achievement, quality of teaching, and behaviour and safety (www.gov.uk/guidance/system-leaders-who-they-are-and-what-they-do).

Heads of teaching schools

The first teaching schools were designated in 2011 with the expectation that they would lead school improvement as part of their leadership of an alliance. To gain the status, schools had to have an experienced headteacher, who had gained an overall outstanding judgement from Ofsted as well as proven experience of collaboration with other schools and of supporting them. Originally their remit was expected to focus on six areas:

- school-led initial teacher training
- continuing professional development
- school-to-school support
- identifying and developing leadership potential
- recruiting and managing specialist leaders of education and
- research and development.

A key aspect of the work of NLEs and teaching school headteachers was to advise government on policy. These roles include membership of organizations such as influential think-tanks, the teaching schools council or reference groups, some of which advised the NCSL/NCTL about professional development. Roles could be temporary or short/medium term (Hill, 2011). Various roles such as school improvement partners have been introduced and then phased out.

Local partnership roles

Such roles as those of executive headship or leadership, headship or leadership of federations, and headship or leadership of MATs are all detailed in Chapter 5 of this book.

In reality, many school leaders have a combination of collaborative roles, which may include two or more of NLE or LLE, leadership of teaching schools, or members of LA boards for school improvement. Higham et al. (2009: 2) suggested that system leaders had taken up new roles made possible through government policy that they were aligning with 'existing local partnerships'.

Characteristics and leadership styles of school leaders engaged in system leadership

Although there are different forms of collaboration, system leaders may have certain things in common, described by Higham et al. (2009: 27) as a 'shared set of characteristics and behaviours'. As school leaders use system leadership to 'embrace new challenges' and opportunities, or 'reinvent themselves' (Matthews et al., 2014: 54), they move from traditional headship to a broader form of educational leadership across schools and localities (Armstrong, 2015). West Burnham (2011) argues that these changes require 'new models and styles of leadership'. Given the varied nature of school leadership and the increasingly complex contexts in which it is practised, there is probably no single theory of leadership that can be applied; several 'perspectives may be valid simultaneously' (Bush, 2008: 8). Robinson (2012: 127) noted that the leadership style of system leaders depended on the 'context and the extent of power, control and influence associated with the role'.

Here we briefly consider those characteristics and skills that appear to be required for the effective practice of system leadership.

Developing a mindset

Craig and Bentley (2005: 3) argued that 'System leadership involves a shift in mindset for school leaders, emphasizing what they share with others over how they differ.' The Innovation Unit (2007: 3) noted that when supporting across schools, it is a mindset that encourages school leaders to 'commit to the learning of every child' and to do what is necessary to achieve it. Robinson (2012: 50) found that all twenty-seven system leaders interviewed had a 'relentless and highly focussed attitude to the pursuit of excellence' and 'intolerance of failure' within, between and across the schools they led.

Motivation and ethical leadership

System leaders need a sense of purpose and motivation, which drives them to walk into the unknown when undertaking roles the scope and consequences of which they do not fully appreciate (Robinson, 2011). It is, however, difficult to identify in any generalized sense what are school leaders' motivations for undertaking system leadership as they may be personal to each individual leader.

Hill (2011) identified several motivators that indicated that heads undertook system leadership to improve their own school and also for opportunities to develop staff and thus improve recruitment and retention. Financial benefits to individual leaders and to their schools were also highlighted, and Robinson (2012) found the 'buzz of professional challenge' the strongest motivator for the heads interviewed.

It is generally recognized that moral purpose with a commitment and deeply held set of values centred on a desire to support children in institutions other than their own is a significant motivator for system leaders (DfE, 2010; Gu et al., 2016; Higham et al., 2009; Hill, 2011; Robinson, 2012). Exercising a form of 'servant leadership' involves, according to Greenleaf (1977), school leaders putting first those they serve and also taking ethical decisions about resource distribution and people management. This seems, as Begley (2009) suggests, highly relevant to leading across multiple organizations.

Ability to influence others

In distinguishing leadership from management, writers have often referred to the influence that helps to define leadership. Cuban (1988: xx) called leadership 'influencing others' actions in achieving desirable ends'. Hill (2011: 13) argues that 'system leadership puts a premium on [system leaders] being able to inspire, persuade and negotiate with other school leaders'. To be successful in influencing others, it is important that system leaders have built a degree of credibility, which is usually gained via external validation or from reputation (Hill and Matthews, 2008).

Collaborative approach

There is clearly an emphasis on requiring a collaborative approach to leadership across organizations, and this is considered specifically in Chapters 3 and 9. There is a 'reciprocal' interdependency involved in 'collaborated leadership' (Spillane et al., 2005: 39) and thereby a need for system leaders to establish trust and good relationships in a variety of contexts.

Resilience

A greater workload has to be managed and with it the development of extra resilience to cope with added demands. Taking on wider roles can change relationships. Robinson (2012) found that many system leaders had an emotional attachment to their original schools and had to manage a sense of loss engendered by reduced involvement in the daily management of their schools and the consequential reduction in social interactions with their colleagues.

Managing change

The way in which headteachers interpret change through their judgement of it, and commitment to it, will affect the way they implement its requirements. System leaders need to know how to adapt quickly to what is needed to 'effect organizational support' (West Burnham, 2011) when putting policy into practice and in new situations. Higham et al. (2009: 2) argued that successful system leaders were able to 'innovate, take risks and deploy resources creatively'.

The ability to adapt to changing circumstances is an important strategic capability as system leaders have to develop their skill base to respond to the context in which they are working (Higham et al., 2009). To manage change requires what Hill (2011) refers to as 'softer' rather than 'technical skills' such as those involved with an ability to communicate with good interpersonal skills and with 'strategic thinking ability'.

Developing capacity and sustaining improvement across schools and the wider school system

Increasing leadership capacity in England and elsewhere relies on the sustainability of system leadership. It is, however, 'fundamental' that the system leader's schools should not be 'compromised' when engaging with the wider system

(Craig and Bentley, 2005: 4) so that collaboration does not have an adverse impact on the school in which they are the substantive leader (NCSL, 2007). Several means have been identified for developing leadership capacity within and across schools and the wider system, which include

- distributing or sharing leadership
- identifying talented leaders and
- capacity building in the wider system.

Distributing leadership

Harris (2009) defined distributed leadership as the expansion of leadership to those who do not hold formal leadership roles or is not 'exclusive' to formal roles (Pont et al., 2008a). As school systems have increasingly used leaders as agents of change, distributing leadership tasks has been encouraged to support the capacity of heads to lead outside their own school in England and in a variety of international contexts, including Australia (Mulford, 2008) and Finland, Flanders and Austria (Pont et al., 2008a). A distributed approach to leadership needs to be suited to the contextual models and practice of the countries in which it is practised (Pont et al., 2008b). In Finland, there are examples of principals of larger schools working at the municipality level and distributing leadership to other staff (Hargreaves et al., 2008), which Mulford (2008) argues that sharing leadership should be an explicit and deliberate aspect of building capacity.

Experience of system leadership in England has led to principals becoming more knowledgeable about how to build capacity in school and on 'preparing leaders at every level' (Hargreaves, 2010: 15). Robinson (2012) found examples of leadership being distributed to senior leaders, including school business managers. As senior leaders stepped up in the absence of the headteacher, leadership was distributed from senior leaders to middle leaders.

Harris (2009, original emphasis) argued the importance of *'how'* leadership was distributed and fully recognized that all shared leadership is not distributed leadership, but can become so if it is accompanied by a degree of formality, empowerment and accountability. Hatcher (2005) noted that the power to share leadership was located in the role of the headteacher, a point echoed by Mulford (2008) when emphasizing the role of the head in facilitating distributed leadership in practice. Robinson (2012) found that many heads were delegating tasks but not leadership until new roles took them away from their schools. Therefore, 'heads were not necessarily distributing leadership by choice but by necessity' (ibid: 128).

Identification and development of talent

The effective sharing of school leadership enabled heads to build capacity in their own schools, which not only enabled them to take on greater responsibility themselves but also to develop other leaders and to retain the commitment of talented staff – a phenomenon recognized in England, and in a variety of international contexts, including Finland (Hargreaves et al., 2008). Building leadership capacity included sharing high-quality leadership development and consistently spreading high-quality practice and ideas (West Burnham, 2011).

Capacity building in the wider system

Barriers to collaboration and system leadership need to be reduced (Greany, 2015). In using school leaders to drive its reforms, a government needs to incentivize them to undertake the roles, and ensure they have the required knowledge and understanding of school improvement to do so (Hill, 2011; NCSL, 2007; West Burnham, 2011). System leadership, therefore, has to be underpinned by high-quality professional development. Formal leadership programmes are not the only mechanism for training, and not all countries that use system leadership have them. Finnish and Belgian system leadership has been essentially 'shaped through practice' (Pont and Hopkins, 2008: 268). Nevertheless, it is important to note the system-wide development that has occurred through the implementation of large-scale leadership training programmes by governments or agencies in different countries. Pont and Hopkins (2008) noted that the leadership training programmes in the state of Victoria (Australia) and in Austria were directly responsible for influencing leadership development on a wide scale. They were aiming to change practice by focusing development to produce improved attainment, and leadership skills hitherto missing. Another example is 'Teach for America', which has a fellowship programme for training system leaders.

In England, the NCSL had been established in the 1990s with the purpose of professionally developing school leaders, and from its early days, it was involved in developing system leaders with its consultant leader programmes and working with networked learning communities. From 2006, the NCSL had the remit to accredit the different 'Leaders of Education Roles', and these roles were discussed earlier.

The refocused NCTL continued to be one of the main vehicles used to drive government reforms, and its latest remit stated support for a self-improving school system that would be led by teaching schools and academy chains together with other outstanding providers. In September 2016, it took greater responsibility for, among other things:

- selection and training of new leaders and
- school-led improvement (NCTL, 2015: 4).

In England, while there is some excellent system leadership taking place, there are also areas where there are few teaching schools or deployed NLEs or LLEs and, therefore, little system leadership accessible for those who need support.

The white paper (DfE, 2016a) recognized this problem and stated that it would 'encourage more leadership development training to be delivered by successful schools' (DfE, 2016a) and included other providers, which, it was hoped, would grow in numbers and in geographical spread. In 2016, the provision in England overall is inconsistent, and recruitment in some areas remains difficult. There is some evidence that system leadership may be retaining talent in schools, but this is not the same as retaining it across the system. To date, there is limited evidence that system leadership has a direct impact on raising standards of attainment (Armstrong, 2015), although there is some recent evidence that pupils in certain federations outperformed a matched sample in non-federated schools (Chapman and Muijs, 2014). It is possible in England that excessive fragmentation of the system means that improvement will be piecemeal for the foreseeable future.

Summary

This chapter has examined:

- the contextual background to the changes needed in the system and the policies that were introduced;
- the reasons why excellent school leaders were seen as central to the required changes;
- the roles introduced to support system leadership and the styles of leadership necessary for its successful implementation;
- the styles and characteristics relevant to successful system leadership; and
- ways in which capacity may be developed and improvement sustained.

Recommended reading

Higham, R., Hopkins, D., and Matthews, P. (2009). *System leadership in practice*. London: Routledge Falmer.
Robinson, S. (2012). *School and system leadership*. London: Continuum.

Chapter 3
The Collaborating School Leader

Introduction

After examining the general context within which various forms of collaboration between schools have come about, and a discussion of the principles and practices of system leadership, we now turn to focus on the school leaders themselves. Whatever the country or context, there are perhaps certain things that anyone in a school leadership role, which involves collaborating with other schools, will need to be aware of. In this chapter, therefore, we:

- briefly discuss the importance of individual school leaders and identify what is involved in effective educational leadership;
- discuss some of the differences that may be needed in leadership between conventional schools and collaborating groups of schools;
- suggest some specific skills and abilities that may be critical in being effective as a collaborating leader; and
- reflect on a possible model for approaches to be taken by leaders of collaborating groups of schools.

Educational leadership and features of effective school leadership

There is, of course, a huge literature on leadership generally, on educational leadership and also specifically on school leadership. Leadership, wherever it exists, can be seen to be concerned with influencing others to achieve certain ends (Cuban, 1988). Linked with this influence is the notion of authority, and the important point to note here is that authority 'resides in formal positions, such as principal or headteacher' (Bush et al., 2010: 3), while leadership can come from anywhere in an organization, whether formally organized or through a natural process. In considering leadership in schools, it is normal to think of those with formally recognized leadership roles, such as principal, vice-principal, a head of a curriculum area, or person-in-charge of pastoral care. School leadership teams commonly consist of persons with formal leadership roles. In terms of overall school leadership, we may consider the following as being some of the generally recognized concerns/features:

- developing a vision for the school;
- developing strategies to achieve that vision;
- influencing and developing an appropriate culture based on values that will sustain those who form the school;
- ensuring accountability to the relevant stakeholders;
- motivating and constantly improving the school's employees/workforce to help raise levels of achievement; and
- ensuring sustainability, especially in promulgating change, by recognizing the significance of the school's context and community.

None of the above is possible unless those people involved in the school commit themselves to these, and leadership only ceases to be an abstract concept when it is seen and heard in the actions, words and behaviour of people concerned. Thus, Harris (2005: xii) suggested that the reality of leadership lies in 'individual connection and personal compassion'. School leadership is essentially a very 'people-focused' business, as an examination of each of the above points makes clear. It seems to us that school leaders, by the very nature of being in the work of education of children and young people, will have a clear moral purpose underpinning both the vision for the school that enables it to have a sense of direction, and the strategies that are developed to enable that vision to be achieved. This moral purpose will similarly influence the way the schools operate on a daily basis, and the values inherent in this purpose, therefore, frame the culture that pervades the school. Such values may be easy to list of course, but, similar to what was stated above, they only become real when they are, for example, overt, explicitly stated, demonstrable and consequential (i.e. leading to action), as noted by Davies (2006).

The accountability referred to is something that in many educational contexts today provides a stressful situation for school leaders, where national government agendas can seem to be, and sometimes explicitly are, at odds with the local, organizational and personal ones of the school and its leaders. The obvious example is where national pressures are on schools to achieve success in what can be seen to be severely limited measurable outcomes (usually externally administered test or examination results), while individual leaders feel they should be committed to education of 'the whole person'. Such dilemmas can lead to leaders being 'terrified of ... the punitive approaches that the Government set for school inspection' (Hammersley-Fletcher, 2015: 204). Nevertheless, accountability remains central to the role of school leadership, whatever the context. Perhaps, as power becomes more shared in the twenty-first century, leaders and other professionals may be able to focus more on listening and interacting (Lumby, 1999) and being supportive of independence and confidence, so that accountability becomes more about being responsive than being 'held to account'.

The motivation and development of the relevant workforce involves a commitment to ongoing training, to research into requirements, to job satisfaction, and all those factors that contribute to people wanting to work there, not least of which may be an admiration for the leaders and their style.

Last and by no means least, the essential feature of sustainability in school leadership requires leaders to recognize a commitment to understanding communities and contexts within which school operate. Most of all, the realization that sustainability is not 'maintainability' but more a commitment to 'change which does not damage individuals or communities but builds capacity and capability to be successful in new and demanding contexts' (Davies, 2007: 23). While a powerful case can be made for successful organizations today to commit to sustainability, the case for schools and indeed other educational organizations to do so is overwhelming, since they are directly responsible for helping to shape the tomorrow's world for the very people they are working with at present – those children and young people who are tomorrow's inhabitants of that world.

This section has tried to set out some of the features of school leadership and some of what it should strive to achieve. These are relevant regardless of the type or number of schools concerned. However, they may show themselves in different ways in different contexts, and some of the potential differences need to be considered now.

Differences between leadership of individual schools and leadership of groups of schools

In a discussion of what makes school leadership unique, different from other educational institutions, as well as from other organizations, Middlewood (2013: 18) suggested at least four things that make schools special:

- their size – they are much smaller than universities and post-compulsory colleges;
- the fact that attendance at them is legally compulsory;

- the fact that their daily 'clients' are children, of ages from the very young through adolescence, and therefore schools have to act 'in loco parentis'; and
- leaders and managers have little time specifically set aside for specific leadership and management activity.

The first and the last of these will be significantly affected by being asked to be the leader of more than school, while the second and third remain at the heart of school leaders' missions, under all circumstances.

Size and scale

Leading a group of more than one school immediately becomes a different job from leading a single school – that much is obvious. Simply the numbers of pupils and parents being greater makes the situation more complex in terms of, for example:

- lines of accountability
- communications
- resources
- management systems
- monitoring and coordinating and
- planning.

Unless these basic organizational requirements are effectively managed, the schools in the group will remain individual schools that 'happen to have' the same leader. Joe was the headteacher of a very small village primary school in an English rural area in the early 1990s, who was asked to also be head of another such school because the then regional (local) authority could not afford to pay two heads' salaries for such small schools. Joe recalls that he was specifically asked not to coordinate the schools in any way, as each had its own identity. He, therefore, shared his time between the two schools with different approaches and traditions. 'It was hugely exhausting,' he said in an interview, 'and a small amount of rationalization would have reduced the workload enormously, but it just was not allowed then.'

The task of coordination of two schools was also faced by principals who had to amalgamate them into a single school, such as two single-sex schools becoming a co-educational one. Kathy had this task in the mid-1990s in the same regional authority and remembers that the focus had to be on the obvious different cultures of male and female institutions being 'nursed' (her word) into a quite different one, drawing on the best of both. She described it as a very 'uplifting and intensely rewarding task, although emotionally extremely draining'. In one case study, Bell (1990) researched the formation of a new school from three previously existing schools, and recorded that the different cultures and histories of the three schools led to intense micro-political activity during the formation period, the consequences of which remained for some time after the new single school was in place and operating.

Such early examples are interesting for the light they throw on issues facing leaders of schools who are required to lead groups of, say, four or five schools in some of the various groupings referred to later in this book. They suggest that rationalizing the various management practices and policies across all the schools, although arduous, may be easier than leading and managing the more intangible elements of schools as organizations – to be discussed later. The size and scale of any rationalization was not the biggest consideration, although the larger the total institution, the greater the need for such rationalization and coordination.

The biggest impact that the greatly increased size and scale of the total area of responsibility can have on the leadership task may be in the area of strategic leadership. Since strategic leadership will involve strategic planning, there is a critical need in looking to the future as much as is possible to be built on a coherent base (Mintzberg, 1995). Such coherence may be much more difficult in a larger and more diverse organization – such as a collaborative group – than in a single, smaller one. In scanning the environment, an essential element of strategic planning, the leader of a group of schools may find discerning a way forward made more or less difficult, depending on the homogeneity or diversity of the schools that make up the group. Global or international concerns may be of similar consideration for all, but more local or regional ones may differ considerably, depending on where each individual school is at present. If we consider the vitally important issue of sustainability, within the group, one school may have been involved in a huge commitment to developing a culture of sustainability, whereas another may have had very little interest in this and indeed could be involved in activities that might be seen by some as actually opposing the principles of sustainability. An example might be that the latter has embarked on a conservation project to save water, but – with a change of staff – had 'lost interest', as Pepper (2014: 514) reported in some schools in Australia. The former has been committed to seeing sustainability as more than conservation, involving itself in community projects that were empowering for future generations. Such differences in philosophy and approach obviously make the setting of agreed strategic goals more difficult, and demand new ways of achieving coherence to be found by the leaders.

Time for leadership activity

If someone who has been headteacher or principal of an individual school becomes the leader of a group of schools, the whole dimension of use of time is immediately transformed. Those who are no advocates or supporters of head-teachers overseeing several schools, such as Mortimore (2013), believe that effective consultation within individual schools is much less likely, and this is certainly a factor to be addressed in any model of such leadership. The role of the executive leader is examined in detail in a later chapter, but here we can note that if an effective leader is one who has a visible presence and is committed to 'walk the talk', then clearly leadership time has to be divided between schools. This may be different in those kinds of collaborative groupings where one school is designated in some way as the leading school (see Chapter 6 on teaching school alliances), but otherwise the leader has some basic considerations:

- Do I base myself in one school primarily?
- Do I give equal amounts of my time to each school? If so, do I do this on a timetabled basis?
- How do I avoid being seen favouring one school above the others?
- How do I avoid my sharing the time out, risking the appearance of superficiality?
- Can I in any real sense be a 'hands-on' leader?

Some of the answers to these and other more difficult questions will emerge through the research into collaborative group leadership presented in Part II. It is reasonable to assume, however, that the leaders of such group will need to strike a balance between being acting as and being recognized as an overall leader while letting others lead on a day-by-day basis in individual schools. Again, the emphasis seems to be on an increasingly strategic role for the collaborative group leader, as already mooted. This transition may be a considerable one for some school leaders, if their previous experience has been limited in that area. Any micro-management is certainly out of the question! Case example 3A illustrates some of the dilemmas in this. It shows how easy it might be for leaders to make mistakes here.

Graham's comments show him being tough on himself, but it is possible to consider whether his brief was sufficiently clear. Was he being asked to get the three schools collaborating effectively, prior to their reorganization into a single school? Was he simply being asked to 'hold the fort' to save leaders' salaries? The purpose of sharing of leadership does not seem clear. In the next section, we stress the importance of being explicit and precise about the purpose of any kind of collaborative action.

Case example 3A

A local (regional) authority in a mainly rural area of England was reorganizing its whole school system in the 1990s, a process lasting about three years. Graham was headteacher of a middle school (nine- to thirteen-year-old pupils) in a relatively sparsely populated part of the area and was asked to take charge of two other schools in addition to his own for the interim period, the other two head-teachers having retired. Looking back, Graham feels he made many mistakes.

> I got just about everything wrong! I tried to divide my time equally between the three schools, and was accused by my own staff of neglecting them. If one school seemed to have a serious problem, I would stay there more and found that problems were exaggerated to get me to stay more! If I found an excellent trainer for CPD days and got them to visit each school, at least one school would be hostile because the other schools had favoured that trainer! Eventually, I felt I wasn't really welcome in any of the schools and found my only peace in stopping in the car on my journeys between schools! I survived and so did the schools until the reorganization happened, when I retired. Looking back, I think what I did wrong was to focus on keeping each school staff happy and not looking beyond that at what was intended to be the point of it all – the benefits for the children. It seems so obvious now of course. I should not have worried about the time allocation but concentrated on the overall direction of the three schools and acknowledged the differences between the schools more.

Skills and attributes needed in effective collaborative schools' leadership

For a group of collaborating schools to be effective, we suggest the members of the group need to:

- have the same moral purpose and the same core values at the centre;
- all be moving in the same overall strategic direction; and
- all be complying with those external requirements that are legally binding;

while ensuring that each individual school group member retains sufficient of its own identity to meet the particular local needs of their learners in their own specific contexts. To enable this, the overall leader may have to be capable of each of the following, some of which may be very different from some requirements of their previous leadership, however effective that was.

- Stop thinking in hierarchical terms. In a single organization such as a school, however distributed or democratic the intention or process may be, the place will be seen as a hierarchy with the leader at the top. This is the person in ultimate control. In any kind of network on the other hand, as Fink (2005: 120) suggests, 'control has to give way to collaboration'. It is no use relying on the role of being a leader; leadership has to be 'earned' (Mintzberg, 2004: 141). This will be discussed in more detail later, but here we may consider the issue of accountability as an example of a change of perspective. In a hierarchy, the leader at the top is the person to whom everyone else is accountable, and is accountable for the school to those who are external to it. We suggest that the model to aim for in an effectively collaborating group of schools is one where the schools that make up the group see themselves as accountable to each of the others for what they do and achieve – we may call this 'mutual accountability' or 'reciprocal accountability'. This may not apply to those models of collaborative groups where one school has been designated in the group's formation as the 'lead school', but should apply in others where all member schools are designated as equal. As far as leadership is concerned, this whole movement may be extremely difficult to achieve in the global educational world where, as Lumby et al. (2008: 466) noted in a summary of international leadership developments and practices, hierarchy is both embedded in most leadership development programmes and moreover 'hierarchy matters considerably in many cultures'.

- Keep the focus on the purpose of the collaboration. The key word here is 'purpose', because the leader needs to remember that collaboration is not an end in itself (although it may be a very good thing!) but exists for a purpose. This purpose is presumably something to do with enabling learner achievement and effectiveness to be better, and certainly better than could have been attained by the schools individually. As we noted in Case example 3A, a lack of clear purpose made the leader's task very difficult. Perhaps a valuable perspective for the leader is to try to see the whole group as a learning organization. Within such learning organizations, the impetus for change and improvement often comes from cooperation with others, both internally and externally, which provides valuable stimuli for all those involved. This way of thinking helps prevent or limit self-interest and serve to remind everyone that they are all concerned with the provision of the best possible education service that can be provided to the learners and those that support them, primarily students and parents. In discussing purpose, it is also necessary to note the essential moral purpose that underpins all education services and to which effective school leaders are committed. Thus, while some collaborative groupings may initially occur because of resources or financial benefits that will accrue, the purpose of the emergent organization, that is, the group, will be the provision of that best possible education service. Evidence from the experiences of education action zones (EAZs) in England in the 1990s showed the benefits, especially to small schools of pooled resources (Woods and Levacic, 1994), but the true effectiveness emerged in the improved quality of teaching and learning in the best of the EAZs. In some countries, where education provision is very unequal, collaboration may be seen as an aid to improving equity of provision of resources, as Mestry (2014) proposed concerning South Africa, but the eventual aim is, of course, to improve the quality of education for all.

- Develop an ethos of trust. Rifkin (2004: 192) explained that because markets are transactions at arms' length, while networks of any kind are about intimate relationships, the former were for self-interest, and the latter shared interest. He concluded that 'markets are based on mistrust, networks on trust'. In any collaborative grouping, effectiveness will only be achieved when the parties involved trust each other, and therefore the leader's task is to encourage and develop an ethos of trust within and across the group. Of course, effective school leadership has often been described as being able to engender trust from those who are led (Bush, 2003; Fink, 2005). In collaborative school groups, the leadership is even more dependent on being able to trust school staffs to operate in an agreed way, because of the more detached role that the leader has. Feys and Devos (2015: 752), in a study of incentivized collaboration in Flemish schools, concluded that 'building trust' was a key skill for leadership in those circumstances. In schools in deprived circumstances, Prew's (2009: 843) research in township schools in South Africa found that shared practices 'built on trust' were more likely to bring about school improvement, while Gillinson et al.'s (2007) work placed trust at the heart of all effective collaborative practice.

As part of building a community based on trust, collaborative school leaders need to recognize that the good ideas can come from anywhere within the group, and not necessarily from anyone in a leadership role. Effective leaders here have the ability to release the positive energy in other people (Mintzberg, 2004), to capture that energy (Slater, 2008), so that potentially everyone can take responsibility based on whoever is best placed to deal with a particular situation at the time.

- Accept complexity as the norm. With hierarchical mind sets rejected, the collaborative school leader recognizes that collaborative systems, perhaps especially so in education, are highly complex ones, and simplistic cause-and-effect relationships do not always apply. This has at least two important implications:
  i. Outcomes can be unpredictable, unlike a 'safe' situation where you know that if you do X, the result will always be Y. Things do not operate in a 'simplistic and linear' way (Bottery, 2016: 30), and this means learning that the future is likely to be even more uncertain than ever.
  ii. Rarely will there be a single clear-cut answer to the complex questions that face educationalists, although this is surely also true of those working in most other fields.

For those in schools, helping and supporting children and young people, such thoughts may initially seem alarming in the context of schools needing to provide them with stability. However, stability is not rigidity, and these children and young people will be living in a world of just such complexity and non-linear understanding and need to be able to manage themselves in such a world. Thus, school leaders need to use the stability of a safe environment at school to help these future adults develop resilience, something the leaders themselves and all school staff equally need at present – as they will in the future!

The collaborative school leader therefore, in accepting complexity and rejecting simplistic, linear solutions, prefers to see problems that occur as being opportunities. They tend not to be afraid of failure, believing perhaps – as Peters (2003: 27) proposed – that 'If nothing goes awry, nothing new can emerge. That is an iron law of nature.' Failure, however, is often defined by those external to the school and who are using criteria that are alien to risk-taking, as they are prescribed by such bodies as national governments and school inspection services precisely to produce single and simplistic answers! Resolving this dilemma may lie at the heart of effective collaborative school leadership. Case example 3B illustrates one school leader's attempt to adopt this point of view.

Case example 3B

This particular example of turning a problem into an opportunity was send to the authors by Belinda, the principal of a downtown school in a city in a western state of the United States. She tells her story thus: 'In this poor neighbourhood, we had considerable trouble attracting good teachers, and sometimes attracting any at all! Most of those we appointed were only mediocre – until, after reading something in Jim Collins's book on achieving greatness in the social sectors, I hit on an idea. I advertised for teachers to teach in a very challenging situation, where the money would not be great, the work would be hard and only the highest quality teachers could possibly succeed. I added however, that competition would be fierce and early application was advised! (This was in a context where we normally received very few applicants and several of these were only moderate.) It worked amazingly! We were overwhelmed, not just with quite a lot of applicants but with many who had first class degrees from top flight universities! We selected some for interview at the school, showed them the situation in all its worst aspects and found them determined to succeed and "Get these kids to achieve" (to quote a typical response!). Importantly, we could not appoint everyone, which meant that the process was seen as selective, a huge incentive for those whom we did appoint and it meant that the following year, we again had well qualified people clamouring for posts – after all, getting a post here was a highly selective process! We have never looked back and I wish I knew how the principle of this could be used to help disadvantaged students throughout the state, maybe the nation. A little bit of me thinks it was sharp practice but if the children gain, I don't care!'

We do not actually see this as 'sharp practice', but as an example of a leader facing a problem and then finding a different way to turn it on its head and seize a chance to improve the overall situation. Perhaps you agree – or disagree?

- Be able to cope with potentially greater personal isolation. As noted earlier, the leader of a collaborative group of schools who is not attached to any one particular school will have a role that is more strategic than operational. This role is also likely to increase the isolation and at times loneliness experienced by principals and headteachers (Barret-Baxendale and Burton, 2009). In describing the advantages of school collaboration in Limpopo province of South Africa, school principals interviewed (Middlewood et al., 2016) stressed the reduction in isolationist feelings as a key personal benefit. Case example 3C describes one such situation.

Case example 3C

Thandi is principal of a primary school in the Limpopo province of South Africa, one generally recognized as the poorest of the provinces. The nearest other school is about twenty-eight miles away with unmade roads giving limited access. She noted that, 'The community the school serves is quite lively and I love the children, the teachers and the parents. I am therefore happy on a daily basis. But when it comes to the big decisions, and dealing with, for example staffing issues, I have a desperate desire to share ideas with someone else who understands. Communications are unreliable and the regional officers try their best but cannot visit very often – when they do, it is a relief to talk to someone! I feel like giving up a job I love sometimes because of this isolation that I feel sometimes. Am I doing a good job, I wonder? Locally, I am told I am, but I need reassurance or challenges from someone at my level.'

Ironically, another principal, Connie, at another school in the same area, and probably Thandi's nearest neighbour, felt the same! She also expressed similar anxieties about not having anyone to share professional issues with and she wanted to stress that this applied to successes as well! Following a programme offered by an English university that highlighted some of the benefits of collaboration, these two principals and one other in an urban context formed a 'learning trio'. While some of the communication was by email (not always reliable), a regular monthly meeting of the three of them was built into the programme, with each school in turn hosting the meeting. Subsequent interviews with Thandi and Connie showed a big reduction in anxiety and stress. Interestingly, the meetings being able to offer practical solutions to each other's problems was only a tiny part of the benefits found. Ninety-five per cent of the benefit was shown to be in improvement in emotional and mental well-being of the leaders.

Similarly, in Tanzania where school collaboration was being proposed in one region, principals there looked forward to feeling less lonely and isolated as being a key benefit (Middlewood et al., 2016). There could be a particular irony here in the sense that, while collaboration between two leaders of individual schools (as will be explored in Chapter 4) can help to decrease a sense of isolation, and this could also be true of collaborative groups of equal and similar schools, the overall leader of a collaborative schools' group may feel much more isolated. That leader has no equivalent person at hand, although developing a network of leaders in such roles could be a solution to offset that feeling. Working with one or more critical friends in similar situations could be highly effective, as long as the terms of the relationship are negotiated and agreed to enable feedback and support to be valuable.

Even with such support, leaders of groups need even more emotional resilience than that which is required anyway of leaders of individual schools who, unlike a deputy principal quoted in Parker with Middlewood (2013: 50), had 'all the excitement and satisfaction of leadership without the ultimate weariness of knowing you are on your own when the buck stops'. School leadership in any circumstances will continue to have elements of being a lonely job, simply because you are the only one in that role in the institution and, therefore, because you carry the ultimate accountability for everything that happens. Collaborating with other leaders of other schools may help to share that accountability in some groupings, may increase it in others, and in certain groupings may make little difference. We stated above the ideal model of accountability to be striven for (i.e. mutual or reciprocal accountability), but meantime the collaborative school leader will need, among other attributes, considerable inner reserves to be effective. While noting all this however, there is some evidence already (NCSL, 2005) that grouping of schools can provide school leaders with more time for reflection and preparation, as well as 'reducing strain and leading to a better work–life balance' (Southworth, 2007: 182).

Reflections on a possible model

In this final section, we try to draw together evidence and suggest that the following might possibly provide some kind of blueprint for the approaches to leading a collaborative group of schools that a leader might find helpful.

- Understanding the context of the collaboration is crucial, not only of the group as a whole but of each individual school making up the group. Given that understanding, the leader may have to learn what Fink (2005: 125) calls 'entry strategies'. These will deepen that understanding and enable them in due course to become an influential part of it. Such strategies will be unique to each collaborative group.

- As noted earlier, the constant focus will be on the real purpose of the collaboration, not on seeing collaboration as an end in itself. Each partner within the collaboration will have its role defined in relation to that explicit purpose. Roles within the group may be complementary to each other to be effective as a whole. For example, one school may have specialist expertise in a particular field, which will be described in its role within the group to achieve the overall purpose. The group as a whole will develop indicators for monitoring the effectiveness of its achieving the purpose.

- Vitally important will be the ability of the collaborative leader to see coherence as the key to the effectiveness of the group, and not see them as number of individual schools put together. This is a complex issue in the educational world in many developed countries where delegation of powers to more autonomous schools has led to greater fragmentation of the system, enhanced by competition. Only a commitment to seeing the larger picture, unified by certain agreed values, will enable the leader to succeed *despite* that fragmentation.

- Because leadership in this context has to be earned, leaders will, as Hodgson (1987) suggested, learn *from* their organizations (unlike managers – who are taught by their organizations) and may ultimately develop a new identity – that of the collaborative leader! This new identity as a leader will emerge after the understanding referred to and probably after constant renegotiation with those involved in the collaboration. The inherent personal qualities of the individual leader, of course, remain the same, but with the attributes discussed earlier, the renegotiation, and the understanding of context and purpose, the collaborative school leader is almost certainly a very different kind of leader from any conventional model that we have been used to. Gronn (2010: 83) suggests that forms of collaborative leadership are likely to prove 'a more realistically grounded alternative to such dubious prescriptions as heroism and distributing the overall burden of work'.

Summary

This chapter has:

- identified some elements of effective school leadership;
- discussed differences between leadership of a single school and that of a group of schools;
- suggested some skills and abilities that may be critical in being an effective collaborative school leader; and

- reflected on a possible model for approaches to be taken by leaders of collaborating schools.

Recommended reading

Bottery, M. (2016). *Education for a more sustainable world*. London: Bloomsbury.
Gronn, P. (2010). Where to next for educational leadership? In T. Bush, L. Bell, and D. Middlewood (eds), *The principles of educational leadership and management* (pp. 70–86). London: Sage.

Part Two

Models of Cross-School Collaborative Leadership

In this section, five different examples are presented, one in each chapter, of research that was carried out in a range of contexts examining different forms of interschool collaboration. Chapter 4 reports and analyses the way the pairing of leaders of two different schools operated, covering both a partnership between state and private secondary school principals, and a model of pairing primary headteachers across several schools in a large city in England. Chapter 5 deals with the groupings of schools in what are sometimes called federations, although, as the chapter explains, different names for such groups may arise as new forms of schools emerge. Chapter 6 describes a specific form of collaborative grouping in England where specific schools are designated teaching schools, and a cluster of schools work with these, with the purpose of raising levels of attainment in all the schools involved. Chapter 7 considers a new form of school called academies, now especially common in the United States and in England and Wales. These academies are linked in collaboration through what are seen as 'chains', again for the purpose of raising attainment, and their nature can be radically different from other groupings. Finally, in Chapter 8, we examine the leadership of those schools where the leader stands apart and operates in an 'executive' role, detached from the day-to-day running. These five examples give an indication of the variety and complexity of the forms that it is possible for collaboration between schools to take, and thereby of the leadership that exists and is needed to take them forward.

Chapter 4
School-to-School Collaboration: Working in Pairs

Introduction

This chapter examines one particular form of collaboration between schools, that of schools working together in pairs. It studies two separate models of such pairing, one between pairs of urban primary schools, and one between a state comprehensive secondary school and a fee-paying private secondary school.

The chapter therefore:

- describes the rationale and context of the project involving paired urban primary schools;
- describes and analyses the findings of this particular project and its possible implications for leadership;
- describes the background to the pairing of the state and fee-paying secondary schools;
- analyses the findings of this project; and
- attempts to draw out and reflect on conclusions and possible implications of the two projects.

Schools or school leaders working in pairs

Paired partnerships for improvement

The notion of people working together in order to achieve greater effectiveness is obviously extremely common. This can take the form of two partners who see themselves as equals, or perhaps where one acts as a mentor and the other tends to be learning from that person during the experience. In these cases, the mentor figure is likely to be someone with a record of greater experience and probably with a record of success in the relevant field. While mentoring is a widely used process and operates at many different levels in organizations, including schools, we are concerned with the process at leadership level. Bush (2008), in reviewing the mentoring of new school leaders globally, found that there were generally a range of perceived benefits for both mentees and mentors. Sundli (2007) challenged its effectiveness in Norway because of the dominance of mentors applying their own plans and values in the relationship. Generally, a need for empathy was stressed as well as the need to avoid the idea that one single solution is possible. Singapore had been a pioneering system in the field with its aim being to provide 'a profound learning experience for the participant' (Chong, 2003: 169). Overall, Bush (2008: 128) concluded that the key factors in the effectiveness of such supportive professional relationships as mentoring were:

- training and prior experience of the facilitator/mentor;
- the matching process; and
- ability to provide an appropriate and individualized balance of challenge and support.

Project of paired primary school leaders

Background and purpose of the pairing

The context was a very large metropolitan city in the Midlands area of England, with a considerable ethnically mixed population and one with some areas of social and economic deprivation, as well as some of relative prosperity. The largest ethnic minority communities of school children are Pakistani (20 per cent), African Caribbean (10 per cent), Bangladeshi (4 per cent) and of mixed heritage (6 per cent). The local authority (LA) responsible for the city was concerned about the underachievement of some of its schools, particularly in those deprived areas, and the various initiatives under the auspices of a newly formed school improvement group (SIG). One of these arranged for the linking of the headteachers of primary and special schools designated 'outstanding' by the national inspectorate with those of schools seen as 'requiring improvement' or 'failing'. The sharing of leadership knowledge and practices, often school to school, was seen as a likely spur to improvement, as argued by Townsend (2011: 101): 'There is a need for leaders to share what they know and what they can do, not only with teachers in their own schools, but also outside of their schools with other leaders from different schools.'

Changes of school leadership took place in several of the schools that are failing or requiring improvement, and later the LA commissioned research into how effective the scheme had been in attempting to raise levels of attainment. The research was carried out by a small team from an education centre in a high-ranking English university. In addition to analysis of data relating to pupil attainment and examination of relevant documentation, the team interviewed the headteachers of ten of the underperforming primary schools and also two special schools in the same category. This sample of headteachers included at least two from each of the authority's four geographical areas of the city. In assessing the effectiveness of the impact on school leadership of the pairing, it was crucial to examine the experiences and perceptions of the leaders themselves. The qualitative data obtained through these was seen as of major importance for the success of any project by which one organization is linked with another, especially in the context of a more successful one partnering a less effective one. The human relationships and responses in such partnerships have been shown to be at the core of their success or otherwise. When the partnership is successful, then if issues occur, 'the problem is in the situation and can be addressed accordingly' (Middlewood and Parker, 2009: 115). The 'collective intelligence' (Lindsay et al, 2007: 5) generated by such partnerships has been found to be powerful, and especially so in the public sector (Williams, 2002). Semi-structured interviews were chosen as the research instrument because they are an 'interpersonal process' (Middlewood and Abbott, 2012: 53), ideal for exploring aspects beyond the specific questions being asked and allowing the complete individuality of each interviewee to be revealed, especially when they all have the same role.

Findings from the project

Key principles in the effectiveness of the pairing of school leaders

Matching of two schools and leaders

The allocation of particular school leaders to the schools perceived to be in need of improvement was initially undertaken by officers of the LA. It was accepted at the outset that these were provisional and subject to acceptance by both parties. In one case, the proposed mentor head did not wish to adopt the suggested school because of what she described as 'personal reasons applicable here'. In the other, the proposed mentee head rejected the other person initially because she felt the circumstances she operated in were 'so very different from the deprived context of this school that I do not feel she will have the right know-how for us'. In all other cases, the recommended mentors were readily accepted, often with enthusiasm such as: 'I knew of her work in her own school so was delighted to think she would be my partner.' Just as Bush (2008) highlighted the matching process as significant in the effectiveness of such pairings, so Barnett and O'Mahony (2008) found that even where the nature, content and format of mentoring and coaching programs differed widely, the way in which the personnel were matched or paired was crucial to their success, and failures were more often caused by incompatibility between the two people involved than any other reason, including perceived weaknesses in the programmes themselves.

In discussing the criteria they hoped to apply to those being asked to work with them, it is interesting to note that the headteachers to be supported stressed that they wanted mentors rather than coaches. They said they were not looking to necessarily learn new skills of leadership and management, although this learning might occur incidentally and, if so, would be welcomed. They preferred to have someone with whom they could discuss issues and problems and draw on their experience, sifting out what was relevant to their own context. While mentoring and coaching are often linked together and can be closely allied and over-lapping, there are differences (Barnett and O'Mahony, 2007; Middlewood and Abbott, 2016), primarily to do with coaching being focused on skills acquirement, as these headteachers identified.

Nature of the partnership

This was widely identified by the heads receiving support as being best seen as a 'professional working relationship'; this was a phrase used by several of the leaders, with its implication that, while a strong personal relationship was helpful and certainly existed in some cases, the stress was on the two words – 'professional' and 'working'. As one leader stated, 'We got on really well, and shared a joke or two, especially as we got to know each other better, but we will not be friends socially; it's all about what you share about doing the job.' Another said, 'As soon as we found we shared the same passion about helping children succeed, which of course is no surprise, we never stopped talking and ninety nine per cent of it was about helping those children.' A further dimension was expressed by another leader who said, 'Without wishing to sound at all pompous, we quickly identified the same moral purpose in our jobs and why we had both wanted to do the job in the first place. We were – and are – both passionate about children's life chances and how to improve them for everyone. That meant, even when we differed over some methods, we knew all along that we both had those same values and purposes in our hearts and minds.'

All these leaders saw 'honesty' and 'integrity' as key elements in the relationship and in the discussions arising from it. All stressed the two-way nature of the relationship or partnership, with a good deal of 'give and take', as described by several. The professional aspect of the partnership was often demonstrated by the mentor leader's suggestion being rejected by the supported leader, usually on the grounds of 'I do not think that could work here in this context because–'. Some of the supported leaders illustrated the two-way nature of the partnership by giving examples of how the mentoring head 'asked MY advice!' and, in another instance, 'She borrowed my school plan so she could use a couple of the ideas in it to show her staff.' In only one case did a supported leader feel that the other leader was 'pushing her own services too strongly', and this was apparently resolved after a 'frank discussion'.

Need for the partnership to be negotiated

After initial introductions, sometimes by the LA officer, the pair of leaders was left to work out their own procedures as to how the partnership could operate for them. All the leaders agreed that there could be no set or rigid rules, but each pair worked out its own way of operating within their own agreed guidelines. Some examples include:

> 'She would never assume she knew the context of my school better than she did.'
> 'She would never assume that because it worked in her school, it would work here.'
> 'No one would make derogatory remarks about staff in each other's schools.'
> 'We would remind each other always to ask for evidence when advancing an opinion about something working or nor working in school. That applied to both schools!'
> 'We would recognize that this pairing was only one part of any overall plan for improvement, and agreed to share ideas about other ideas to help when they cropped up.'

Identification of supported school's needs to be done jointly

While analysis of the weaker school's situation had clearly been done previously, both by national inspectors and by LA personnel, all the leaders recognized that a key factor in the success of the new leader would lie in their having their own opportunity to analyse the situation and contribute to proposals for improvement. As one noted:

> The worst thing would have been for her (the mentor headteacher) to have marched in here and said, 'Now what you need to do is so and so.' I needed to have my own ideas, have read the reports, and then sit down and share them with her, listen to her ideas as well as mine and come to an agreement about what was needed. I particularly felt I should lead on the priorities, because you cannot do everything at once, and I knew what I felt I could achieve most readily first. She agreed and said I needed some relatively easy successes early on, so that became our first strategy.

Such an outlook was strongly felt by all the supported leaders, and only one instance was noted where a mentoring leader was felt to be advocating her own remedies, through use of her own school resources, too strongly. As another leader shrewdly noted,

> If it goes wrong, I will not have the luxury of blaming the other person! She allowed me to decide for myself and I learned massively in the process. In fact, sometimes I would ask her what she would do, and she would always say 'Tell me first what you think should be done'. So I would tell her, then we would discuss it, criticize it and so on and only afterwards did I realize she had never told me what she would have done! That taught me a lot about the reality of leadership!

Need for agreement about resources

However positive the relationships, all stated that there needed to be agreement about what resources, financial and otherwise, were likely to be involved and what expenses could be incurred. The importance of this lay not only in sound economics but in the need to avoid the embarrassment of rejecting an idea on the grounds of cost. Expenditure, therefore, was regularly monitored.

Recognition that other sources of support were important

All leaders, in both roles, were clear that this initiative was by itself not a panacea for the improvement of the unsuccessful school. Several other factors came into play, such as professional development of staff, parental involvement and effective use of resources. However, many of these were identified via the discussions between the two paired leaders, and in some cases, the 'other' school became involved in training, staff exchanges and other forms of development.

Two specific case examples now help to bring out some of these issues. Case example 4A is of a supported headteacher.

Case example 4A

Claire (not her real name) tells how she felt about the pairing as it began and how things developed.

> I obtained the post in May and the previous person had been 'encouraged' to retire! I knew the school's position as a failing school and had read the inspection report as well as the Authority's own report. I was told that an experienced head of a successful school would be paired with me for my first year. I met her in fact in July, just before the summer holidays. I naturally looked her and her school up and felt a bit intimidated before we met because of her record of success. However, I was ambitious and was determined not to be pushed around by anyone, because I was clear what I wanted to do! I need not have worried since, as we met, I saw she was not the pushing around kind! Her first words were basically, 'I'm sure you have lots of ideas about making things better here. Do you want to share some of them with me?'
>
>   We got on really well and although I was resolved to do my own thing, I found myself asking her opinion a lot. Her normal response was 'Well, what do YOU think first?' Where she clearly thought my idea was not any good, she would say, 'What do you think the implications for so and so might be?' and I would consider something I really hadn't thought about. I got out of any habit I might have had to ask her what she might do, because we agreed that every context and each set of persons is unique. I began to realize that my personal leadership style was likely to develop over time and that however pleasant I wanted to be, there were some things in the early days 'up with which I cannot put' – to coin a phrase. Sometimes, she said, 'Well, if you do that – which of course you can – do you think that so and so might happen?' It helped reflection, even if I determined to go ahead. She never said 'I told you so,' if anything did not quite go as I hoped. I think we both knew that such a remark would be the end of our relationship as it usually is in life in any relationship!

The perspective of the mentor or supporting head teacher, Eileen, is given in Case example 4B.

Case example 4B

> I became an NLE, and this was the first time the Local Authority had asked NLEs to pair with leaders of failing schools. All the NLEs had a meeting together first before going to the schools, and we had a broadly common approach, whilst recognizing the individuality of each school and its leader. I got the impression that the Authority wanted a fairly prescriptive approach, but we were all experienced leaders and were well aware of why this might not work.

I met Claire in July before she started in September, after I had studied her CV and previous experience. On our first meeting, I felt her potential to be slightly resentful of me if I were to be too assertive, but I remembered myself in my early days of headship – where I didn't have this kind of support by the way – and made sure I went softly. We actually got on very well, and although I thought a few of her ideas were in danger of making things worse not better, I recalled my own resentment at my ideas being dismissed in my early days, and found a way of getting her to see some of the potential drawbacks to an idea. On one occasion, I remember she laughed and said, 'What you really mean is that this is a daft idea, don't you?' We both laughed and she said that it probably was daft, and she'd save it for a later time when the school had improved. I felt she could use her more assertive side in the early days to be quite tough as some staff had become complacent and even lazy! In other words, her style could adjust after the initial more authoritative stance of early days. I got regular feedback from other sources about her progress and it was really heartening to hear how she and the school developed and that I played a small part in that. A mistake I made was that my approach here would also apply to my next one – but that is another story!

Reflections on leadership from the project's findings

From this research into pairings of primary school leaders, it may be worth reflecting briefly on what common principles appear to be present across the various examples.

- Developing as an effective leader is not a matter of learning specific skills in a conscious way, such as through set programmes or courses. It may be an assimilation of others' approaches and experiences.

- Context is all-important. Leaders who are effective in one context will not automatically be so in a different context. Where they are, it is because they have certain inherent abilities that they can adapt to different circumstances. 'Leadership is bound in context, but while it does not lend itself to recipe swapping, discussions about common ingredients can be helpful' (Riley and MacBeath, 2003: 184).

- However much sharing occurs, school leadership can ultimately be a solitary role that has a specific accountability.

- Effective school leaders learn to 'be themselves', and their individual style needs to be able to grow and develop as they make it their own.

- However experienced a leader may be, learning will continue and enable the leader to develop continuously.

- Most importantly, school leadership is always underpinned by a deep moral purpose related to the betterment of the children or young people for whom the school exists.

State and fee-paying school pairings

This project involved two separate examples of a fee-paying secondary school being paired with a state secondary school. In both cases, access was more easily gained to the state schools than to the fee-paying schools, but it is felt a picture emerges of the perceived issues within the pairings from both partners. While the fee-paying schools both had primary units attached to them, the research focus was on the secondary phase for purposes of comparison.

The first example involved one of the most prestigious and notable single-sex fee-paying schools in England being paired with a highly successful co-educational secondary comprehensive school in a relatively affluent urban environment. The paring was entirely voluntary, received no separate funding and came about through a contact at a conference, which led to the two principals initially agreeing to a student exchange. While there are several very important aspects of this exchange that are of great interest in terms of different school cultures and expectations, our focus here is on leadership. After a fairly 'explosive' beginning to the student exchange, when a group of boys from the fee-paying school misinterpreted the lack of uniform at the state school as an opportunity for laxity and were found smoking on site, the exchanges went well with students being made very welcome in both schools. One fee-paying student said, 'I just thought it would be a skive, hence the smoking, but after a period there, I am in awe of the students at X because I am certain that if I spent two years here, I would fail my A Levels!' This comment on the two different regimes in operation at two highly successful schools in terms of examination results reflects on the leadership of the cultures of the two places. Each principal visited the other's school and expressed respect for the different ways in which success was achieved. Roger, principal of the state school, said in an interview,

> The schools are so far apart in history and culture that all the things I believe in and am committed to are in quite a different form there. Tom [the other principal] could never understand why everyone was so much less deferential to me in walking round the school than happens at his place. There, when the principal is on his 'rounds', students and staff tend not to speak until they are spoken to, whereas my lot come up and tell me things – always politely. I have worked at this and I am sure Tom feels the same in his school but it is SO different! My worry about the fee-paying school's culture is that there still persists the two cultures deep down – maybe not that deep! – one for staff, one for students. As far as I am concerned, the values to be exhibited must be the same for everyone, although expressed in different ways in adults and younger people. I think Tom might say the same, and after all, perhaps it is what the parents who pay large amounts of money to send their sons there expect and hope for.

One of the most striking differences between the schools noted by Roger was in the area of student voice. Roger's school was noted for its radical student involvement in student research, students reporting to leadership and governors and having a big impact on curriculum development and school policies. He was slightly amused to see Tom's pride at what Tom felt was real student democracy, which involved one student per month being allowed to speak to a body with the principal about a school issue to be addressed. 'Perhaps it is a start, but what we do would not be tolerated in Tom's school,' was Roger's comment.

Reports from students of both schools are fully recorded in the various newsletters and governors' reports of the state school but, perhaps interestingly, not in the equivalents of the fee-paying school. Here, the visits and exchanges are reported factually with dates and numbers and so on. It is reasonable to assume that this reflects the difference in importance attached to the exchanges by the two schools. As far as learning about school leadership from the links between the two schools, Roger was clear.

> I learned nothing that I could take on as useful and I am sure Tom would say the same! The situations are so different. Tom's school starts with huge advantages in terms of history, facilities and resources of course and we also have excellence in those areas, except being able to call on notable and wealthy old boys to donate them! My gripe of course is that in this country (England) national governments are far more likely to take note of what Tom or his successor says about education than what I or my kind say. That is the nature of the impact that private education has on our whole education system – it is a political point, and I do not apologize for it as over ninety per cent of children are in state schools and only the rest in one's like Tom's. When you hear ministers say they want all schools to be like the best private ones, you fear they are so out of touch, we are always battling against policies rather than feeling we are supported by them.

The second example of partnership between a state school and a fee-paying one was also from England, this time in the northwest of the country; both schools were secondary and the state one was co-educational and the fee-paying one a single-sex school. This came about through the government's official scheme encouraging such partnerships, originally established in 1998 and organized by the DfES and the Sutton Trust. Although the official aims of the partnership are to share resources, including expertise, both the principals interviewed felt that it had not worked in their case. Mark, the state school principal, was quite scathing but also honest about the idea in the first place. He said that he could not see that any independent school anywhere near us will have anything to offer us – except we play them at sports! When asked why he joined the partnership scheme, his reply was,

> I tried to be fair, I think. I was against the whole principle because it seemed to be set up on the premise that private schools could help us state schools

improve. Michael Gove (the then Education Secretary) talked about them lending us an expert teacher for example and the head of a private girls' school I know was scathing about that also, saying she did not have teachers twiddling their thumbs in the staff room. Although the principal I was paired with was a perfectly nice person and we had some interesting chats, my original belief was confirmed and we parted amicably after a year! As far as leadership is concerned, our philosophies of education are so far apart that I could not feel I could gain any insights through looking at how the other half live. I could not do his job because it represents everything I stand against!

The perspective of Peter, the other principal involved, is given now. Peter's views were that he also found the partnership a failure but attributed it to the inbuilt prejudice on Mark's part, meaning that the partnership never had a chance of success. His views on school leadership are given in Case example 4C.

Case example 4C

Our approaches to leadership of our schools were quite different, although it seems we are both seen as successful! The figurehead part of my role is extremely important. When parents choose us as the school for their sons, they look hard at the headmaster to see if he will uphold what they think the school stands for and the values he will help to instil in their sons. Those values include being ambitious and determined to succeed in life, compassion for others, particularly those with fewer advantages, loyalty, a sense of order, self-fulfilment, and as much as possible social justice. I support these and try to model them – although of course I fail sometimes as a fallible human being! Mark's school has its own values and many are the same, I know, because we discussed school values. The difference is in the way they are lived and shown. When we discussed justice, for example, Mark saw my school predicated on a basic social injustice of one rule for the haves and another for the rest. I start from an individual's right to have a particular education for their children if they prefer that. It is nobody's fault, I suppose, that it did not work. If we had been paired with a failing state school, it might have worked, but I know then patronizing would have to be avoided!

I was really interested in Mark's way of running the school, but it is not transferable and could not work here. I felt that he was so inherently opposed to private education and schooling – which is his right to hold that view, by the way – that our partnership could not work in the sense of learning from each other. Maybe there are things we can do, such as sharing resources, but it is too late now.

Some brief comments on private and state school pairings

Both our examples of such pairings were from England, where the independent/state partnerships initiative (Ofsted, 2005) has had very mixed results, and our examples seem not untypical. Australia has reported on more successful such pairings (Groundwater-Smith and Mockler, 2003) and criteria for effective collaboration set out. However, these placed no emphasis on leadership, except that effective collaboration needed leadership support. In some countries where private schooling plays a significant part in the nation's system, such as Greece or The Netherlands, few examples appear to exist. As noted earlier, the relative failure of the two pairings examined – in leadership terms – stems from widely differing concepts of effective education that inevitably influences the kind of school leadership that is seen to be required in each of the two different sectors. As Begley (2010: 52) notes, the perceived 'purposes of education must be at the forefront as guides to decision making and strategic planning. They are the meta-values of the profession'. Only then can you have what he calls 'morally defensible educational leadership' (ibid). It is possible that such mutual opposition in their ideas about purposes of education meant that the individual leaders involved were unable to see even minor aspects of leadership in action that might have been transferable and possibly beneficial.

Conclusions and reflections on collaborative leadership through working in pairs

Effective collaborative leadership here seems likely to depend on several factors:

- The collaboration is voluntary; attempts to force collaboration or even to significantly incentivize it (Feys and Devos, 2015) are much less likely to have benefits for schools or leaders.
- The acceptance of mutual learning is seen as central; where one leader is either actually or perceived as 'superior' with nothing to learn from the other, then the collaboration between leaders will be ineffective.
- There is mixed evidence about the role of a third party or agency to facilitate collaboration. Clearly, much depends on who that agency is, and how it is perceived by both leaders. In some cases, this can involve the extent to which the agency brings resources to aid the collaboration (Feys and Devos, 2015).

- There is recognition that there is no single correct way and that the effectiveness will emerge through both partners working their way through the professional relationship to develop individual leadership approaches and styles. In a modern context in developed countries of targets, assessments and fixed structures, the question to be asked by leaders, as Collins and Porras (2011: 201–2) suggest, is not 'Is this practice good?' but 'Is this practice appropriate for us – does it fit with our ideology and ambitions?'

- Collaborative leadership is likely to work better in an environment where those involved are not seen as in direct competition (Stevenson, 2007).

- The model of more experienced leader working with a new school leader can have valuable implications for both parties and the future leadership of the new leader. Not least of the gains may be in the experience of the new and younger leader learning that if an older and more experienced person listens to what they say, they will probably listen to others in the future who may be even less powerful than themselves (Gold, 2010: 39).

Finally, all the other chapters in the section examine collaborative leadership in much larger groups of various kinds. Given the evidence here, is it possible to suggest that school leaders working in pairs, if effectively managed, might be a valuable way in which they can develop appropriate experience to enable them to move on to leading these larger collaborative groups?

Summary

This chapter has:

- described the collaborative model of schools working in pairs;
- described the findings of a specific research project of paired school leaders and analysed these;
- reflected on the implications of the analysis;
- described two examples of pairings of private and state schools and reflected briefly on the findings from those pairings; and
- tried to draw conclusions about school leadership through pairing.

Recommended reading

Bush, T. (2008). *Leadership and management development in education.* London: Sage. The section on the mentoring of principals describes the variety of practice in many countries and examines the key principles involved.

Hayes, G., and Lynch, B. (2013). Local partnerships: Blowing in the wind of national policy changes. *British Educational Research Journal*, *39*(3), 425–46.

Chapter 5
Leadership in Federations: Working across Trusts and Groups

Introduction

This chapter considers how a range of school collaborations in England, with federation and multi-academy trust (MAT) status, has affected the kind of school leadership needed there, and the advantages and disadvantages of this.

The chapter therefore:

- describes the background of federations and MATs and the reasons they were established;
- briefly describes the types of collaborative structures researched for this chapter;
- analyses the impact of the role of the leader of a federation or MAT on their leadership practice and on other leadership in their schools;
- examines the extension of leadership across schools;
- considers the advantages and disadvantages of federations and MATs;
- notes how the federations or MATs may evolve and create a sustainable future; and
- offers some reflections on leadership of federations and MATs.

Background of federations and MATs

Chapter 1 gave information about the growth of collaborative arrangements for schools in various countries. Early federations in England were usually set up as an arrangement first brokered by the local authority (LA) where the rationale for their creation was led by the need for school improvement or succession planning where headteachers were difficult to recruit (Chapman et al., 2011; Wood and Simkins, 2014). Difficulty in recruitment was also a reason for federations being created in The Netherlands (Collins et al., 2005).

A 'hard' federation was the term used in England for where the schools concerned had one governing body. This involved the formal use of the term 'federation' and had legal status. Some were a loose collaborations between schools and referred to as 'soft federations' because they did not, other than establishing some shared committees, formally share a governing body. West-Burnham (2011) refers to these as 'collaborations', one example of which he cites as sharing leadership or leadership support. The term 'soft federation' for this form of collaboration has generally fallen out of use in the literature, but can still be heard in practice.

In a white paper (DFES, 2005), the UK government signalled its intention to encourage the growth of federations in England as part of a strategy for system leadership. Chapman et al. (2009) described the range of federative structures as:

● 'cross-phase', which included schools from different age ranges;

● 'size federations', which are often horizontal such as the forming of a federation of small rural primary schools;

● 'mainstreaming federations', combining special and mainstream schools;

● 'academy federations', which are a combination of schools with the link to governance of a sponsor or chain; and

● 'faith federations', which consist of a combination of faith schools and may or may not overlap with the above.

MATs are structured in different ways. These can be national chains similar to the Charter movement in the United States in being publicly funded state schools, and these national chains can act as sponsors of schools. Other MATs offer more local provision, sometimes involving a teaching school (see Chapter 6 for a fuller description and discussion of teaching schools). Both the national and teaching school chains have been encouraged by government policy in England to sponsor schools deemed vulnerable to failure, requiring improvement or special measures, according to Ofsted. Umbrella trusts exist where an overarching group such as a diocese creates within it a MAT that is accountable to the diocese but has a separate funding agreement and articles of association, subject to agreement by the Secretary of State.

Chapman (2013) suggested that the term 'federation' was being superseded by the term 'MAT'. By the time of the publication of the white paper of 2016 (DfE, 2016), federations were mentioned only in connection with a named federation that was also a multi-academy trust.

Salokangas and Chapman (2014) have noted that tracking and monitoring the progress of chains of academies in UK is limited, compared with a greater understanding of the development of charter schools in the United States. Tracking progress and development of chains and federations in England is difficult, because of the rapid change that happens sometimes where the size and nature of the collaboration can change by the week or month (Hill et al., 2012).

Federations and MATs in this chapter

MATs and federations have largely been created to suit 'local conditions' (Kerr and West, 2010; Wood and Simkins, 2014), and all of the eight structures described in this chapter reflect this. Although the extent to which arrangements were permanent or temporary, fixed or fluid differed between the organizations, all were initially set up as 'performance federations' (Chapman et al., 2009). (Note that all quotations come from the federation or MAT leaders interviewed for this chapter.)

Table 5.1 shows the basic details of the sample used for this chapter.

A is a diocesan MAT, which is formed of one secondary school and eleven
   primaries with four more expected to join shortly. It was formed as a
   response to perceived potential school failure

At the beginning, it [the MAT] started with schools that were either in special
measures or had just come out of special measures. It was 2 or 3 really
vulnerable schools that were at the risk of losing their C of E (Church of England)
status because they were going to have to go to other sponsors. – Linda
The only thing the schools have got in common is me! – Linda

B is a primary federation comprised of two schools within the same local
   authority. It was formed following a good school's support for a vulnerable
   school. The federation later converted to become part of a sponsored MAT.

C is a federation that developed from the beginning within a MAT. Originally
   Brian's school was a 'forced' academy conversion to a sponsored MAT,
   when the school was in special measures.

D is a rural federation of two small lower schools, which was formed both
   as a response to the crisis at the time in recruitment and also to improve
   standards in the second school. Case example 5A describes this journey.

Table 5.1 The sample used for federations and MATs

Leader	M/F	Role title	School status	Number of schools in organization	Context
Mike A	M	Executive headteacher	Federation/MAT	Two secondary schools and one middle school	Small town in north central region
Nigel B	M	CEO	MAT	Five children's centres, four primary and three secondary schools	Suburban and inner city central region
Lynne C	F	CEO	MAT	One secondary and four primary schools	Inner city central region
Martin D	M	Executive headteacher	Federation within a MAT	Two primary schools	Inner city central region
Linda E	F	Executive headteacher	Collaboration within a diocesan MAT	Two primary schools	Inner city central region
Brian F	M	Executive headteacher	Federation with a MAT	Three primary schools	Inner city central region
Sarah G	F	Executive headteacher	Collaboration within a MAT	Variable	Inner city southern region
Wendy H	F	Executive headteacher	Federation	Two primary schools	Rural central/south region

Case example 5A

The federation comprises two schools approximately five miles apart in a rural part of the south midlands in England.

The current executive head, Wendy, was appointed to an existing 'soft federation or what should be called a collaboration'. She believes that the reason the federation was created was because one school was unable to recruit a headteacher. As an interim measure, the head of a local school, who was shortly to retire, ran the two schools, while the LA tried to find another headteacher. Wendy states that 'the previous head did not run the schools as a federation at all but as two separate sites and there was no collaboration happening between them'.

After the head retired, an interim head was appointed as the schools were still struggling to hire a head, eventually needing three rounds of advertising before engaging Wendy.

Initially governors wanted a head who would have a teaching commitment as well as leading the two schools, which Wendy considered unrealistic. Eventually, it was readvertised as the soft federation in Wendy's words 'to make it more appealing'. She was tempted by the role because 'the governors were behaving as if it was a federation. It was a slick glossy advert with the name of the two schools and federation across the top. It was clear that two schools were working together'.

Unfortunately, however, she laments that 'when I came here and met the staff it was clear that it wasn't two schools working together at all!' As the schools distrusted each other, leading them was a real challenge but one she relished. There were two governing bodies that were very distinct and ran things in different ways, with a working party between the two.

This situation changed over time, and now the schools are far more recognizable as a federation. There is one governing body, joint curriculum planning and considerable collaboration between staff in the different schools.

Wendy leads a maintained school federation within the LA and has no desire both philosophically or pragmatically to change the status of her school. She notes:

> We don't want to be academy and fully funded. We get very well
> supported by the LA for funding and building work and we couldn't
> afford it any other way. I count in the millions the amount these two small
> schools have had spent on them in the last 7 years. We'd never get that
> elsewhere. Funding is an important issue for remaining an LA maintained
> federation because small rural primary schools are not considered viable
> for sponsors to be interested in taking over.

E, F and G are school-led MATs. They have grown from federations, often of two schools, to become larger organizations. In F and G, the outstanding school that formed the basis of the initial federation became a designated teaching school.

All three of these MATs are vertical federations of different phases, a format that was seen to have innate advantages. In E, the collaboration was between two secondary and a middle school.

I think the horizontal federations are less powerful than the vertical ones. I know from experience that secondary schools learn more about teaching and learning from primary ones, and the primary schools in the model can benefit from the subject specialism offered by the secondary school. – Mike

F: This MAT developed from a federation when an outstanding secondary school federated with a vulnerable secondary school and the federation grew to include a primary school. The outstanding school gained teaching school status and the federation grew in numbers, eventually becoming a MAT. It is a complex MAT comprising five children's centres, four primary schools and three secondary schools, one of which is the teaching school.

When I started there were 7 schools and the structure is that each school has its own headteacher and there is genuine autonomy. – Nigel

This MAT has a much wider circle of influence through its networks, including another twenty-two schools acknowledged as part of the alliance.

G: This MAT has one secondary school, which is the teaching school, and four primary schools, and Case example 5B traces the background to how this MAT was formed.

Case example 5B

The road to becoming an MAT started over six years ago when the principal of an outstanding secondary school became an NLE and supported another secondary school in special measures. She became executive head for a part of the week supporting the existing principal. There was a trust set up in the other school and she was chair of the trust. When the school had a 'good' inspection judgement, she moved on while appointing an acting 'head of school' at her own school.

Following the success of her work, it was decided that she should continue to work as an executive head and to retain the role of head of school, albeit with another incumbent. This was based on the fact that the school had gained teaching school status and her workload had now become substantial.

Later, it was decided to set up a MAT 'because there wasn't one in the LA'. It took over two years from getting the academy order to setting up the trust because, 'the LA was opposed to them doing so and the politics and legal bits conspired against them' (Lynne).

There are currently four primaries in the MAT, and 'We are suddenly taking off big time. More with primary and it's likely we'll have a good little batch of primaries joining in the autumn. We try to do it on a 2–1 basis of 2 good or better to one that needs support' (Lynne).

Within the MAT, it is felt that the primaries work well as an autonomous group. One of them is an outstanding school and has an executive head who was persuaded to be executive head of a school in special measures, and her outstanding school has also come into the trust. A deputy from one primary has been moved to take over another, and the executive head of the outstanding school leads that as well. Therefore, the primary executive head leads three of the four primaries. While the MAT has five schools (four primaries and the teaching school), Lynne leads a complex structure of wider collaboration. She is trying to ensure that 'the TS works in tandem with the MAT but the group of people we work with varies at any time'.

H falls within the definition of soft federation because the chair of governors from Sarah's base school has also become a member of the governing body. This is not a permanent arrangement and is expected to change after one year. This is a very fluid situation as Sarah also leads executively in other schools in the MAT and was considering a hard federation in the not-too-distant future.

Leadership in federations and MATs

The circumstances in which leadership is practised are changing with the introduction of federations and MATs, but the importance of leadership to their success is uncontested.

An analysis of the variation in the different job descriptions of executive leaders, why some are deemed executive headteachers/principals and some are CEOs, why school leaders would choose to become executive leaders, their motivations and characteristics are dealt with in Chapter 8. This section, therefore, only describes the roles of the executive leaders in relation to how that leadership is *practised* and *distributed* to ensure the organization is effective, together with the impact this has on others and the organization.

New and varied school structures and networks create new patterns of relationships and ways of working for school leaders, which leads to differences in leadership practice. Some of this practice inevitably changes with the movement from leadership of a single institution to leadership of multiple institutions. In addition, leading a federation of two or more schools that is maintained by the LA will have different leadership responsibilities from those of one operating within a sponsored MAT. A further complication is the difference between the role of a chief executive or executive principal leading a chain of schools in a school-led MAT as opposed to the leadership of a small school-led federation.

The amount of power to make decisions and shape local circumstances exercised by an executive leader working within a multiple organization can depend not only on the job they operate with but also the influence they may be able to wield as a result of their perceived success and value to the organization.

The roles of CEO and some highly strategic executive headteachers and principals have a strong correlation with the role of superintendent in The Netherlands as outlined by Collins et al. (2005). These include responsibility for controlling federation or MAT budgets, vision for the whole organization and compiling a strategic plan. This was often compiled in conjunction with a board of members from other schools in the group, such as in three of the eight researched.

All the federations or MATs employed the use of an executive headteacher who led strategically but also had a range of operational leadership responsibilities. These varied from being highly operational in the day-to-day work of each school, to having no management responsibility, but still being the named leader overall for a school or schools, to being a CEO across a number of schools with no responsibility for an individual school (according to the DfE's Edubase, which is the register of educational establishments in England and Wales).

Wendy undertook both executive leadership and coordination of support for children with special educational needs and disability, albeit with the support of an experienced higher-level teaching assistant for two mornings a week to support her. In addition, she undertook all the project management for estates. She had little opportunity or inclination to delegate.

> If I'm not here but in the other school, there isn't someone who can step in because the deputies are full time teachers. I am still very much the headteacher and called on all the time. Very 'hands-on' still. – Wendy

Linda and Sarah are still very closely involved in the day-to-day management of the schools they supported as it was part of their contract to be so and the schools needed considerable leadership support. Sometimes close involvement was a result of their inclination as professionals rather than necessity due to lack of resources. Mike wished to combine both: 'I have to be a bit of everything and enough of everything for people to know I still care. If you can get that then you've won.'

As the organizations grew or developed to become more effective overall, the operational aspect of those who had previously had a larger hands-on role had to change to reflect the contextual needs of the school. This often involved a move away from operational to a more strategic role.

> I have had to step back as I'm not as hands on as I was. Being a head in a rapidly improving school meant that I had to be able to write those RAPs (rapid improvement plans) and be involved in every pupil progress meeting and modelling lessons etc. I still think all of that is important but I don't have time. – Martin

As these leaders, especially of large complex multi-phase structures, found the strategic role dominated, and they were less involved in the operational life of the organization, it was important that they were reported to, as they monitored and evaluated the progress, effectiveness and success of the organization and its constituent parts. For Nigel and Lynne, any operational activity in the school was severely curtailed by the range of strategic work they undertook on behalf of their organizations nationally and locally (see Chapter 8 for more detailed descriptions of job roles). The extent to which the leaders were involved operationally affected the extent to which they felt they needed to be visible. School leaders were actively choosing the sort of role they wanted and developed their organizations at least partly to accommodate this. Unless they chose to be, those leaders who had stepped away as CEOs had little need to be visible to parents or children. For some, being visible was a conscious choice.

> Since September there have only been 3 days when I haven't been to every school every day. That's on purpose. – Mike
> Visibility is very important and making sure that I'm going to be visible in both schools enough. – Martin

There was a general consensus that leadership involved hierarchy within the MAT or chain, with an overall principal or CEO leading a defined structure. Both Lynne and Mike were adamant that 'flat MATs' would not work, because there needed to be an overall leadership perspective.

Extension of leadership

Changes to the leadership role of the school leader when they undertook the leadership of a multiple organization had consequences for the roles of other staff. These include:

- changes to staff roles and
- how leadership was distributed within and across the schools.

The degree of autonomy for leadership decision making distributed to staff and the control held by school leaders or the governance of the trust was variable.

All, however, stressed the importance of building a collaborative culture in their organizations. This was especially pertinent when changing the working practices of staff who had been used to working in one school rather than a multiple unit organization.

> When I started there was a lot of resentment about the process because it wasn't a collaborative but a 'done to' process . . . we have done a lot of work about building teams and creating teachers' teams and working together building classroom support teams which have an opportunity to work across

both schools. CPD is run jointly . . . At all levels there are partnerships and people
meet and plan with each other. – Martin
Staff work in partnership and not in isolation . . . The first development plan was
with all the staffs' inputs and so they knew immediately I wanted to work in a
collaborative way. –Wendy

Changing staff roles

New roles were created to facilitate the increased leadership demands on the
federation or trust. Where there was an executive headteacher/principal, there
was a range of roles that supported them. Four of the eight were supported by
headteachers/principals in the federated schools. Three others had deputy heads/
vice principals. The range was dependent on the perceived contextual needs of
the organization, including the structure leaders had inherited.

A comparatively new role that is now growing in the extent of its use by
executive leaders is that of 'head of school'. These roles are more strategic and
have greater responsibility than deputy heads but do not have the overall strategic leadership role of the executive. Being a head of school was considered to
be good leadership experience and preparation for executive headship.

Traditionally, there was clarity about the definition of the terms headteacher,
deputy headteacher and latterly assistant headteacher. With the increasing range
of multiple organizations, there arose some contradictions and potential confusion over the use of terms. Chapman (2013) noted that the increasing demands
of the external roles of heads led to a 'shift' in the responsibilities of deputy
heads. This in turn can lead to changes to other senior leaders' roles. There is little consistency in the responsibilities that holders of these roles have in practice.
One CEO had appointed directors of primary and secondary phases, and these
two postholders were appointed from the seven headteachers within the MAT.

New and revised roles often necessitated new contracts for staff, and these
were sometimes and increasingly federation or MAT contracts, which expected
teachers to be deployed in any school in the organization if necessary.

Most of the contracts are still with the individual schools; there are some
federation contracts and all the ones that have been issued since I've arrived are
federation contracts and state that you have to be prepared to work across the
schools. – Mike

Shared leadership

Distributing leadership can be a mechanism used in the leadership of single
schools particularly if they are large and indeed; 'distributed leadership' is a

term widely used – and still debated – in the relevant literature. It is, however, particularly important as a pragmatic response to the leadership of new multiple organizations where the 'top-down' approach closely associated with single school leaders cannot be sustained. Leading more strategically usually meant that some leadership tasks had become more widely delegated to senior staff. This action involves issues of autonomy and control according to the degree to which leadership is distributed and the parameters that exist for independent decision making or use of initiative by staff and, as noted by Hatcher (2005), the control that remained with the overall leader of the organization. This is, however, more complex in a multiple organization CEO that includes the roles of principal/headteacher of each school. While the ultimate authority lies with that person, there will be more levels within the hierarchy and, therefore, a greater need for clarity regarding the remit of roles and distribution of leadership tasks.

Distributing leadership involves an element of stepping back and allowing others to lead.

> Sometimes I have to take a step back. If there was a problem in an individual school I could just go and fix it, but I should say to the head 'Have you thought of this and that' so I don't undermine him/her but also that I don't let things slide or help him/her not to make a mistake. You have to make the judgement almost on an individual basis. – Mike
>
> I give the heads confidence. They make decisions but I can lead them in how they make them and what they think about so I can challenge their thinking but it is very much a case of my saying to them 'this is your school'. – Linda
>
> I have to have confidence in them and allow the principals to make decisions. I could tell them what to do and maybe I should in certain circumstances but I want them to be able to make mistakes. – Brian

All recognized the importance of building relationships and of knowing the strengths and weaknesses of their staff. The key elements were consistency in approach and good communication.

> The danger of being an executive head is that popping in can undermine people even if that is happening unintentionally. I always say that I will be responsible for this, this and this in a school and then the other bits are yours and you can come back to me on things. – Sarah

Most of the leaders of extended organizations did not want to be involved in micromanagement, and they trusted the relevant staff to 'get on with it'. It exasperated some of them to be asked about how to deal with something that they felt was an area they had delegated to others.

The distribution of leadership by school leaders was often a pragmatic response and enabled them to build capacity in their schools to free them to lead elsewhere. Thus, executive leaders were able to undertake CEO roles and particularly become more involved in leading at a national level. Many executive heads actively encouraged their staff to work as system leaders both to retain them and to support those in need. In Case example 5C, Martin describes some of the system leadership undertaken by his federation.

Case example 5C

In [a vulnerable school in the MAT but not in the same geographical location], we were supporting with the maths progress and teaching. We established a maths leader and team, and maths champions throughout the school. We did what was necessary to improve it throughout the school. In another which is not part of our MAT I supported a new head with how to establish a school improvement cycle and monitoring.

Establishing the basics. I've been involved in quite a few schools sharing our assessment system and the processes and benefits of it.

And it's not just me. Initially it was just me but I've learned such a lot from going out to schools that I know it will improve leadership in others. Currently the Maths leader from [School X] is working as an assistant principal to support another school in the MAT which needs leadership support. Two other staff have been supporting a local school down the road for Early Years. We've run our own moderation sessions and local schools outside the area have come to that. Our Literacy lead has been supporting other schools too. It's not a case of just me, but our leaders do a lot of system leadership supporting in other schools.

Leadership for sustained improvement

Leadership for sustainability was a priority. Some leaders, such as Linda and Sarah, knew they were on fixed term contracts and had built in succession planning with the coaching and leadership development for their successors. Sustainability was an issue because many of the heads had developed highly individualistic organizations built around their personal skills, particularly the large teaching school MATs. Lynne was typical:

> Depending on that (funding) bid, there will probably be enough money to appoint a deputy CEO with a view to succession planning. No one currently around the table wants my job.

Hill et al. (2012) suggest that successful chains have a relentless commitment to school improvement and that quality assurance measures could be found that worked across a particular organization. This both enabled a consistent approach and mitigated risk. Executive leaders interviewed had robust internal quality assurance measures sometimes coming from heads of other school organizations in the form of peer review or companies they employed to assure.

Mike, for example, tried to 'ensure quality by getting someone who used to be a DfE adviser who will come in and assure what I'm doing'.

Externally imposed quality assurance, other than Ofsted inspection judgements, depended on the type of organization. Sponsored MATs have quality assurance procedures through the establishment of regional directors, and teaching schools have some quality assurance as part of their remit.

Advantages and disadvantages of leading in a federation or MAT

Advantages identified were:

- *economic*, using finance and pooled budgets flexibly across organizations and generating income by selling services;
- *professional learning* opportunities and development;
- *system leadership and opportunities to build capacity* across the organization and beyond; and
- *recruitment and retention* of staff.

Economies of scale

Chains of schools and federations in England accrue larger budgets than single schools due to their size, which helps them to offset any increase in the costs of the structure or management of systems, such as payroll, HR, IT, finance and estates management (Chapman et al., 2011; Hill, 2010; Hill et al., 2012).

Sponsored MATs deduct a portion of the total budget (known as 'top slicing') before allocating funds to their schools; this is then used to create core services for those schools. Offering these services across a number of schools reduces the cost to individual schools through economies of scale. This is also found in other kinds of MATs.

> The budget funding comes into the single trust pot and then goes out to the three schools, but we keep 4% which pays for my salary and a few other development projects across the schools. – Mike

Salokangas and Chapman (2014) found that economies of scale and centralized 'back office' functions were often key reasons for joining an academy chain. Economies of scale were noted across a range of organizations

> Procurement is a major advantage for us of the federation. I can say to builders we need a classroom and 3 miles away we need a hall. We can get a better deal. – Wendy

Income generation

School-to-school support usually comes with a cost. This is often offset within MATs as being something expected to be done for the 'family' either at cost or a reduced rate or as a reciprocal arrangement. It would have been difficult to reduce or discontinue system leadership and retain the roles and capacity built up.

Income generation for some heads was hampered by their commitment to support as part of their moral duty to support all children. Wendy, for example, charged little for the behavioural support she gave to a local head she was mentoring as it was part of her style to be supportive, and she put this above income generation.

Professional learning and CPD

The structure of federations or MATs enables professional development to be delivered across a group of schools, thus taking advantage of economies of scale (Chapman et al., 2011). Improved opportunities for professional learning were highlighted as an advantage by all eight interviewees. A federation or a MAT can offer professional development tailored to the need of the organization or individual schools within it and delivered more cheaply. Also, by being 'in-house', it was more likely to lead to sustainable improvement and more consistent practice and pedagogy; many larger MATs offered their own leadership development programmes.

Small rural schools benefittfed from cross-organization profession development as, due to their environment, there is a danger that they can become isolated within their community.

> For us as two rural schools the advantage of federation is that we are not as isolated as the staff work in partnership. – Wendy

System leadership and building capacity

Internal system leadership can be identified as support offered to other schools within the federation or trust, and was noted by Hill et al. (2012) as being a practice widespread in sponsored chains. Working as a collaborative group enabled experts within all of the schools to work across the organization. This was particularly important in performance federations where professional learning was used to help raise performance in weaker schools.

> Being a federation helps school improvement dramatically. It helps to spread expertise and there are people to bounce ideas off if things aren't going well. – Brian

Successful support for other schools provided professional satisfaction and validity.

> Obviously working with other varying levels of leadership in other schools has given me some recognition that some of the things we do here do work elsewhere – which is some validation for our way of working. – Martin

Through system leadership, these organizations build capacity in the wider system while ensuring that they do not reduce capacity internally

> Having the structure that we have has allowed us to reach out into the community and across our schools and beyond to really effect change and influence whilst still ensuring the fires are burning back at base. – Nigel

Recruitment and retention

In a small school, there may not be many opportunities to staff for career development. Being a larger organization however gives MATs or large federations the advantage of being able to retain principals and other staff or promote them internally. This is a phenomenon noted by Hill et al. (2012) where they found 25 per cent of sponsored chains promoted internally for the role of principal. Five of the eight leaders interviewed had promoted leadership roles within their collaborative organizations.

Salokangas and Chapman (2014) noted that the culture of collaboration and opportunities to be involved in the strategic planning and shaping of MATs were retention mechanisms. In our sample, wider strategic involvement included the chance to be on MAT boards for areas such as standards or for attendance at high-level meetings.

Brian felt that there should be more of a mapped-out career path for executive heads as part of the strategy for retention devised by his sponsored MAT. The idea of a career path has some resonance with the leadership development in chartered management organizations in the United States where leaders work a form of apprenticeship before they are appointed as principals (Lake et al., 2010).

Retention of staff by being able to offer them experience across a range of organizations was a strong inducement for recruiting and subsequently retaining staff that all eight recognized. As noted by Chapman et al. (2011), leaders felt that they were giving staff opportunities for leadership pathways they otherwise would not have enjoyed.

> Between the two schools there's more opportunities for progression … people can be refreshed working in the other schools in a federation when otherwise they might have left. – Martin
>
> I can think of two members of school that have been promoted in school and developed and work in one of the other schools … That way we (the Federation) have kept two high quality people. – Brian

Disadvantages

Lack of shared vision

In Dutch federations, Collins et al. (2005) noted several disadvantages, which included balancing the needs of the schools and those of the federation over-all and potential problems caused by a lack of shared vision. The hierarchical nature of federations and chains in England makes the issues of shared vision less likely as the vision may be collectively discussed but is ultimately controlled by the head of the collaborative organization.

Leadership of the executive being stretched

Work intensification, particularly as federations and MATs develop, was highlighted as potentially being a disadvantage. This was especially true for the rural federation where the head could not afford non-teaching leadership support.

> Disadvantage if you don't thrive on a challenge is the workload. Since I took on the second school I haven't had a summer break because of the building work, which I project manage. Every summer is taken up with another building project … I save money that way. – Wendy

An intensified workload also led to issues of time management and visibility.

> It's difficult to divide your time as an executive head … It's learning what to prioritise … if you take your eye off the ball, things can change. – Brian
> The downside is the amount of time you can realistically give to each school. – Sarah

Managing the scale of the organization

A potential disadvantage was for the organizations to grow too quickly through popularity and become, in Mike's words, either 'a beast' or 'too insu-lar' with a silo mentality. In addition, the power and kudos of building a suc-cessful organization can lead to negative reactions on the part of the executive leader.

> People can think that as an executive head your motives are empire building. It's like having a spear and standing at the top of a hill! The danger is that it can get too big and maybe some people do get too big for their boots. – Mike
> The executive head can't have an ego especially if it's a negative ego and they have to be committed and not just see the role as a stepping stone to something greater. As a teacher you come in with an educational philosophy and sense of moral purpose and you shouldn't lose sight of that. – Linda

Evolving federations: creating a sustainable future

The executive leaders were all involved in horizon scanning for new initiatives to help improve their organizations and for ways of ensuring school improvement and a sustainable future. Many of their ideas involved growth and change.

> Our group strategy is to look maybe at clusters of schools particularly as we get bigger because communication will become challenging. It may be that we work in more small clusters of schools. – Nigel

The diminishing role of the LA was recognized, and only Wendy was looking to them for any form of support. She would not leave the LA as a maintained school because of the security it gave to small rural schools. The others, however, identified that the LA was unable to offer them any form of sustainable future.

> I think in the future there will be more teaching schools and MATs. Some will work and some won't. – Lynne

Overall, all eight expected the number of MATs and federations to increase, in some part because of the scarcity of principals and headteachers, regardless of the advantages anyway of working collaboratively across schools in various forms.

Reflections on leadership in federations and MATs

The type of leadership in evidence in federations and MATs is much more diverse than in single institutions:

- The executive leaders were all previously successful as heads of single institutions. Is this experience a necessary prerequisite for executive leadership? Is it an appropriate one?
- Leaders of small rural primary federations are more operational due partly to necessity but also sometimes from choice.
- Economies of scale are an advantage for all leaders of federations and MATs, but smaller federations gained less from economies of scale than the larger ones.
- Leadership practice and the development of the organization as a whole in terms of growth and development was heavily influenced by the personal inclination of the school leader.

- Workload has intensified for all leaders, but there were differences in the type of work, ranging from greater operational loads for heads of small primary schools to a greater strategic leadership and national role for some of the executive leaders.
- Some federation and MAT leaders are very influential at national level because of the success of their schools and that they are working at the cutting edge of knowledge and research.
- Executive leaders are trying to build system-wide capacity and actively ensure the future sustainability of their organizations through the recruitment and retention of high-quality staff with leadership potential. This is achieved through providing a wide range of opportunities and system leadership.

Summary

This chapter has:

- described the background of federations and MATs and the reasons they were established;
- briefly outlined the organizations used in the research sample;
- analysed the impact of the role of the leader of a federation or MAT on their leadership practice and on other leadership in their schools;
- examined the extension of leadership across and within schools;
- considered the advantages and disadvantages of forming federations and MATs;
- noted how some of the federations and MATs expected to evolve and create a sustainable future; and
- offered some reflections on leadership of federations and MATs.

Recommended reading

Chapman, C. (2015). From one school to many: Reflections on the impact and nature of school federations and chains in England. *EMAL*, *43*(1), 46–60.

Higham, R. (2010). Federations and system leadership. In A. Hargreaves, A. Lieberman, M. Fullan, and D. Hopkins (eds), *Second international handbook of educational change* (pp. 725–39). New York: Springer.

Chapter 6
Leading Teaching School Alliances: Working in Hierarchical Groups

Introduction

One of the collaborative initiatives that was briefly considered in Chapter 1 was that of the teaching school alliances, which were initially established in 2010 as part of the drive by the UK government to create movement towards a self-improving school system. The teaching schools were introduced at a time when many of the school support and development functions previously carried out by local (i.e. regional) authorities were being cut, as the government moved to make schools ever more autonomous and free from external authorities. The teaching schools have taken on a number of those functions and established alliances with a range of partner schools. In this chapter, we consider the reasons why teaching schools were established and describe and reflect on their growth and impact. It will draw on data collected from a research project, undertaken by the authors, in a large metropolitan authority. This chapter therefore:

- considers the background to the establishment of teaching schools;
- describes the development of the policy;
- identifies aspects of good practice in successful teaching school alliances;
- describes the findings from a research project investigating teaching schools and school improvement; and
- explores the role played by the headteacher/principal and senior leadership team in the establishment of effective school leadership.

Background

Teaching schools have been in existence in a variety of forms for a number of years. They were a feature of the London Challenge, which was referred to in Chapter 1 and similar initiatives in a number of English regions. Berwick and Matthews (2007: 2), in a paper advocating the establishment of teaching schools, argued they are 'schools which are deliberate and successful learning communities, akin to teaching hospitals'. They go on to develop the comparison with teaching hospitals:

> The teaching school is less identifiable than the teaching hospital. Rather than it being another type of schools with another type of rationale, it is a conceptual idea involving a **commitment to managing your knowledge by growing your own and sharing it with others.** If we understood the principles behind success, everyone might find it much easier to run their schools. In London, schools have been faced with a huge tapestry of different innovations; what is needed is a linkage between schools that provides greater coherence. (Berwick and Matthews, 2007: 18)

Teaching hospitals are highly regarded by the medical profession and by society at large and considered to be leaders in their field. While health provision has been subject to similar competitive pressures found in other parts of the public sector, the relationships between teaching hospitals with other local hospitals is, however, very different than the situation between schools in a local area. Schools, for example, are likely to find themselves in much more competition with each other for potential students. Teaching hospitals also have much closer formalized links with local higher education institutions that play a significant part in the training of doctors and other health professionals (Gu et al., 2016). In teaching schools, these links are less developed and, in some cases, virtually absent. Nevertheless, there are some similarities between the teaching schools and teaching hospitals:

> Modelling teaching schools on teaching hospitals is an idea whose time has come. What started as a proposal to the Cabinet Office (Berwick, 2004) became a pilot in London form 2005, followed by participation by some schools in Greater Manchester and elsewhere before becoming a government policy commitment in 2010 . . .
>
> There are clear parallels between the concept of teaching schools in England and teaching hospitals. Teaching hospitals have a strong commitment to teaching and research, alongside and through the medical services they provide . . .
>
> Many prospective patients would see treatment at a teaching hospital as an advantage, just as parents seek out good schools. This is because patients perceive that teaching hospitals are centres of clinical excellence, with access to

leading-edge research and highly trained staff whom they can expect to receive the best possible medical attention. (Matthews and Berwick, 2013: 9)

Across the world, there are examples of similar types of schools to the teaching schools that have been established as leading-edge schools designed to develop and promote best practice. In the United States, there are the laboratory schools that have the following features:

- exemplary practice
- research and innovation
- a resource for teacher training
- professional development and
- wider influence. (Matthews and Berwick, 2013: 10)

Many countries, for example, Australia, Canada and Thailand, have demonstration schools. In many cases, these schools have close links with local universities and are designed to showcase exemplary practice. In Finland, there are training schools that play a significant part in the training and professional development of teachers. In England, over 200 training schools were established as centres of excellence for initial teacher education and continuing professional development. Despite the apparent similarities with teaching achools, there is a significant difference between the training schools, the international examples we have given, and the teaching schools currently operating in England. The teaching schools in England have a wider remit in terms of school improvement, and the significance of working in collaboration and developing partnerships with other schools is a major part of their activities (Gu et al., 2016). In fact, as we describe below, the new teaching schools incorporated the training school elements when they were established. At the heart of this whole process is the drive to raise standards and bring about school and system improvement through the establishment of a self-improving school system – see, for example, Hargreaves (2010, 2014). The ultimate intention is to create a system where social capital is created in schools as they develop their own improvement systems, which can then be developed into broader collaborative capital that is capable of being shared across a system:

It describes a state where strategic alliances between schools are commonplace, where collaboration-cum-competition is the normal and natural way in which the system operates, and the principles and practice of system leadership are widely shared. In a system with collaborative capital, the power of the schools' social capital to support the sharing of intellectual capital and to generate new intellectual capital increases sharply. The system evolves a new system capacity; the knowledge and skills of collaboration in alliances accumulate to create a new form of capital. (Hargreaves, 2011: 26)

Development of the teaching schools policy

In 2010, the UK government embarked on a radical reform of the education system (Abbott, Rathbone and Whitehead, 2013). Building on work initiated by the previous Labour government, the new administration were influenced by policy initiatives from around the world, especially developments in a number of Scandinavian countries and the United States. The white paper 'The Importance of Teaching' (DfE, 2010) set out the major areas of reform. According to Abbott et al. (2013: 182), 'the title of the White Paper is intriguing and suggests that the teaching profession is seen as central to the government's aim to improve the education system'. Writing in the foreword to the white paper, the then prime minister and deputy prime minister identified three key aspects of the English education system that required attention:

> The first and most important lesson is that no education system can be better than the quality of its teachers . . . The second lesson of world-class education systems is that they devolve as much power as possible to the front line, while retaining high levels of accountability . . . The third lesson of the best education systems is that no country that wishes to be world class can afford to allow children from poorer countries to fail as a matter of course (DfE, 2010: 3–4).

This last point underlines that the elimination of inequality in educational provision and standards was essential and the self-improving system was ultimately to help raise the level of achievement of ALL children to that which existed in the best schools.

The white paper identified seven broad policy areas that would require reform to enable the development of a world-class education system:

- Curriculum, assessment and qualifications through review of the national curriculum and changes to existing examinations;
- school funding by introducing a more equitable system;
- student behaviour policies by giving headteachers and teachers increased powers;
- accountability through reform of the school inspection system and reporting process;
- school improvement by shifting the emphasis to individual schools and the extension of national and local leaders of education;
- teaching and school leadership with an emphasis on initial teacher training and continuing professional development; and
- school system through the creation of new types of school and the extension of the academies programme.

As part of the process to achieve this radical reform of the education system, the white paper proposed the establishment of a number of teaching schools:

> We will develop a national network of new Teaching Schools to lead and develop sustainable approaches to teacher development across the country . . .
> More recently, in London and Greater Manchester, the model of a Teaching School has been developed, modelled on teaching hospitals. They are outstanding schools led by outstanding head teachers [national leaders of education], which have a track record in improving pupil outcomes through supporting other schools.
>
> We intend to bring together the Training School and Teaching School models to create a national network of Teaching Schools. These will be outstanding schools, which will take a leading responsibility for providing and quality initial teacher training in their area. We will also fund them to offer professional development for teachers and leaders. Other schools will choose whether or not to take advantage of these programmes, so Teaching Schools will primarily be accountable to their peers. We intend there to be to be a national network of such schools and our priority is that they should be of the highest quality – truly amongst the best schools in the country. (DfE, 2010: 23)

More specifically, the teaching schools have six main areas of responsibility, and these are often referred to as 'the big six':

- school-led initial teacher training
- continuing professional development
- school-to-school support
- identifying and developing leadership potential
- specialist leaders of education and
- research and development.

The identification of six major areas of activity has placed some pressure on the teaching schools in terms of delivery and reach. However, it seems clear that for these to be achieved, the individual teacher has to be at the heart of each of 'the big six'. The intention is to raise the overall quality of teaching and learning in schools through the activities instigated and developed by the teaching school, which can then cascade throughout the teaching school alliance. Case example 6A gives an illustration of how this can happen in practice.

Case example 6A

In a borough of London, a teaching school alliance has a particular emphasis on special education and inclusion, and the principal of the teaching school, Ahmed, feels strongly about how the alliance can make a big contribution to this important field of education. According to him,

Schools everywhere, both special and mainstream ones, need leaders who are committed to high standards for ALL children and who can ensure that the school staff feel the same. In this school and throughout the alliance we place stress on inclusion, ensuring that future leaders can come from any background. We offer training throughout the alliance schools and focus early on in recognizing unintentional prejudice and how to face it and eventually eliminate it. We emphasize that this is not a missionary zeal issue, but to do with equal opportunity and ultimately raising levels of attainment for everyone. Within the alliance, we use transfers, fixed term secondments, job swaps and job shares – all to help people gain experience and insight into a range of contexts. The focus is very much on staff and improving their skill levels. At the end of the day we want the best possible staff who have had the opportunity to develop their skills. We are fortunate that the area covered by our schools includes ones with multiethnic populations, rather mixed social class ones and even two single sex schools. When you have tested your values about inclusion in such a variety of contexts, you really know whether you have those values for real! Communication is also key to us in the alliance, and our trainers and mentors really do need to have their fingers on the pulse! I don't mean to make it sound as if we here do all the training – we don't. It comes from any school but of course, different schools develop their own strengths and specialisms so we know where to go for the best provision. One of the overarching leadership roles is in monitoring that there is not an excess of staff movement as we need to remember all the time that the pupils in the schools are the most important people and their learning must be disrupted as little as possible otherwise the whole exercise becomes counter productive.

The original target set by the government in England was the designation of 600 teaching schools by 2016. The government then achieved this target, and by February 2015, there were 692 teaching schools representing 538 teaching school alliances (Gu et al., 2016). There were clear criteria for designation as a teaching school, although these have been refined to ensure equal coverage, so that every school could have the opportunity to benefit from working with a teaching school, no matter its geographical location. Originally designated schools had to be graded 'outstanding' in their most recent external (Ofsted) inspection. According to the 2016 eligibility criteria, schools have to have an Ofsted grade of at least 'Good' for overall effectiveness, leadership and management, and teaching and learning or quality of teaching. In addition, those schools eligible in those respects still had to have a track record of:

- demonstrating sustained high pupil performance and progress over the last three years;
- having senior and middle leaders who were rated as outstanding;

- delivering high-quality school-led initial teacher training;
- providing evidence-based professional development opportunities for teachers and leaders; and
- providing school-to-school support to spread excellent practice.

Also to be eligible to apply to become a teaching school, the headteacher or principal had to

- be judged to be a good serving headteacher with at least three years headship experience and expected to remain at the current school for at least two years following designation;
- be accountable for one or more schools that meet the teaching school criteria; and
- have the full support from the schools' governing body and a reference from a commissioner of school-to-school support (NCTL, 2016: 2).

Teaching schools and school improvement

As has been pointed out earlier in the book and in this chapter, there has been increasing pressure on schools to collaborate to bring about improvements in education. Enabling and encouraging schools to share resources and to improve professional has been at the heart of this process in a number of countries. In the teaching school alliances, schools have been able to develop their own level of involvement, and many have increasingly secured ownership of the changes that have been introduced (Muijs et al., 2010). In this section, we consider a case study of how in one local authority area, schools contributed to the development and operation of a number of teaching schools.

The context of our study was a large metropolitan city in England, which has considerable areas of deprivation alongside areas of relative affluence. The school population consists of a significant proportion of students from ethnic minorities. At the time of the research project, the role and influence of the local authority, which previously had been proactive in terms of providing a wide range of support and monitoring services for schools, was declining, and schools were gaining greater autonomy. The city had enjoyed national prominence for the quality and extent of the support provided by the local authority. This was becoming a distant memory as the school system started to fragment as different types of school and school groupings were established. A number of teaching schools had been designated as part of the new school arrangements across the city.

The intention of the study was to include perspectives from teaching schools and the schools they were working with. In particular, it was intended to consider the attitudes and perceptions of the school leaders towards the alliances that had been established and the various roles within them. The study aimed to:

- establish the principles underpinning the process;
- identify the range of activities taking place;
- explore the role of participants, especially senior leaders;
- evaluate the effectiveness of the process;
- identify factors contributing to effectiveness; and
- make recommendations to improve the process.

There is considerable evidence that shows that the effectiveness of any partnerships or alliances between organizations depends heavily on the quality of the relationships between the personnel involved, especially the leaders and/or the managers of those organizations (Frost, 2005; Todd, 2007; Williams, 2002).

The study consisted of three parts. Initial documentary analysis was undertaken to study policy documents and individual school policies. Second, semi-structured interviews were carried out with a number of local stakeholders, including the head of school improvement and the chair of the local education partnership. The third phase of the study consisted of visits to primary and secondary teaching schools and other schools in their alliance. Semi-structured interviews were conducted with senior leaders in the schools. As argued elsewhere, semi-structured interviews are an ideal method to explore a range of perspectives, including the human issues that may underpin particular leadership practices (Middlewood and Abbott, 2012).

Findings from the study

A number of issues emerged from the study:

- Senior leaders in the teaching schools were keen to stress that 'moral purpose' was a major factor in their decision to become a teaching school (Fullan, 2003). In particular, the need to make the individual child at the centre of everything was felt by them to be central to everything they did. There was a strong belief from senior leaders that they were working in successful schools and they all felt they had a responsibility to support other schools to help them improve. In particular, they were concerned about the decline of local authority services and saw that there was a need to help to fill the resultant gap to bring about system-wide improvement. However, teaching school leaders were reluctant to assume too many of the responsibilities of a local authority; one headteacher commented that they 'were definitely not taking on the Local Authority role'. It seemed on further inquiry that this leader was concerned about the image of an external authority as being somewhat bureaucratic and 'top-down' in style, being transferred to the teaching school when this leader was very clear that in no way was this their role. The leader felt this perception would significantly and adversely affect their relationship with other schools in the alliance.

- Effective communication between all schools in the alliance was identified as a key factor in its effectiveness, and establishing good relationships between school leadership teams was an important part of this process. Positive staff who were committed to working with other schools were of vital importance to ensure the success of this particular collaborative initiative.

- According to all those who were interviewed, there are a number of key criteria that determine effectiveness of the leadership of this type of initiative; these included:
  a. ability to respond quickly to developments and policy initiatives as well as to local difficulties or problems, such as a failed school inspection or a sudden resignation of a key person;
  b. ability to identify areas of concern by 'picking things up' quickly and also to be aware of hidden issues;
  c. in particular, utilizing the skills within the teaching school and, where appropriate, other schools to identify and resolve issues;
  d. ability to become involved in a range of development and monitoring activities, being able to be flexible rather than just focussing on one particular specialism;
  e. ability to have a strong focus on the central importance of teaching and learning;
  f. ability to develop effective professional relationships at school leadership level;
  g. ability to select appropriate and committed personnel to be involved in links between schools at all levels;
  h. ability to appoint additional staff, either teaching or administrative, to support the activities of the teaching school;
  i. recognition of the difference between monitoring and support (given the nature of many teaching schools' leaders, this is difficult because they often wanted to support other teachers in less successful schools);
  j. a willingness to be 'tough' where there were areas that required drastic improvement, including addressing weaknesses in staffing and also in management;
  k. identification of the relationship of each school and leader with the local authority; and
  l. provision of adequate funding to facilitate development activities. Many activities were expensive especially in terms of staff time, and schools had to have sufficient resources to be able to carry out remedial activities effectively and sometimes quickly.

- Overall school improvement and improved outcomes for students were seen as the measure of success of the teaching school alliances, as far as these interviewed leaders were concerned. One headteacher of a teaching school commented, 'This is an interesting process and it demands a lot from me and my staff. However, it's also given my school and our staff lots of opportunities to be involved in a whole range of activities, but it is impact driven. If things don't have an impact and bring about improvement, we have to ask why are we doing it?'

Leadership in teaching schools

One of the key themes throughout this book has been the importance of leadership in developing successful collaborative approaches. The 'moral purpose', which was discussed in the previous section, is an example of system leadership, and there is strong support for the claim that even in a market-led education system facing competitive pressures, many teachers and especially headteachers still have a strong commitment to helping and supporting other schools that are less successful and that need to improve (Matthews and Berwick, 2013).

Senior leaders in teaching schools have a crucial role to play in their development and success. They have to establish a clear vision and structures within the alliances that will enable the schools to work effectively together. There will be a need to ensure consensus on the more important developments, and this is often achieved through developing effective relationships with leaders of other schools in the teaching school alliance. The leader of the teaching school also has to ensure that standards do not fall at their own school and ensure that staff are not distracted from maintaining the high standards that led to the award of teaching school status in the first place. It can be a difficult balancing act for senior leaders to sustain this in a period of change. There has to be some degree of sustainability of policy and leadership, and a collaborative rather than a top-down approach is likely to facilitate this process:

> A school partnership approach to school improvement, as seen in the work of many teaching schools and NSSs, is typically based on a collaborative leadership structure, one in which there is clarity at all levels about what is to be achieved … The most effective leadership partnerships have several dimensions, they are most concerned with providing support and building knowledge through coaching, mentoring and brokerage. (Matthews and Berwick, 2013: 49)

There are occasions when the relationship between schools is not productive; and in Case example 6B, we recount part of an interview with a headteacher, Wendy, who was unhappy at the perceived lack of support from the teaching school.

Case example 6B

Wendy is the headteacher of a catholic primary school in a city in the east midlands in England. She was attached by the local (regional) authority to a group of schools working with a designated secondary teaching school. When interviewed, Wendy expressed some doubts about the worthwhileness of the group from her perspective. She said,

> I don't make any use of the so-called alliance. Our school is seen as an outstanding primary and as such we do all we can to work with and where necessary help other schools. We, along with two other local schools, one of which is a nursery school, share ideas and we three headteachers meet regularly. I've never really got on with the headteacher of the Teaching School. Very different ideas and to some extent values. Patronizing is a word I would use, there are others! Only one of those other two local schools is in the alliance. We see ourselves as a triad, and supported by the local Diocese, because we are all Faith schools. It is a much more natural home for us. When we want specific help, it is to the Diocese we go and they are very supportive. To be honest, I haven't found the Teaching School has much to offer us and in any case, being a secondary school, I don't think they know what our needs are. We actually have another primary school from right across the other side of the city that is interested in joining our triad – obviously we won't be a triad then! The better or even ideal situation for us would be for a catholic school, primary or secondary, it doesn't matter, to be a teaching school and be at the centre of an alliance based on that school. After all, we would all have the same values then, and it seems to me that if a collaborative group is to work, it has to be based on shared values. I can guarantee that my staff and my parents all feel the same. Looks like we're going to have to apply to become a Teaching School!

There are several issues for consideration here, reflecting on the relationship between the teaching school leader and Wendy. Perceptions seem to play a large part in the weakness of this relationship. How might it be improved? Who should take action? What leadership approach is called for?

While this book is focused on a collaborative approach to leadership, it would be erroneous to assume that collaborative approaches necessarily mean consultative at all times! Evidence and the literature makes clear that leadership at times requires a more direct and 'top-down' approach. This is often associated with particular and often long-standing problems in schools, where a sea change is required to shift people from a comfort zone, which has led to underperformance or being satisfied with being just 'good enough'. See Middlewood and Abbott (2017: 113–18) for a full discussion of this issue. It is worth reflecting here on the need for occasionally a more robust or tough approach to leadership that, it can be argued, can be found in some academy chains where a 'one size fits all' approach has been more developed. The word 'chain' perhaps by itself implies something very different from the word 'alliance'! Chapter 7 explores this particular collaborative structure.

One of the biggest difficulties found by leaders of teaching schools in showing leadership of the alliance was in establishing the difference between monitoring and support of other schools in the alliance group, as noted briefly earlier. Given the background of the school leaders concerned, some felt it was in their nature to go in and support a school where they perceived weaknesses, and some felt their initial brief was not sufficiently clear on this. Others were clear that their task was to monitor what was happening and not to take direct action. The research found examples of both the tough direct action, described above, and also of a more detached monitoring approach from some leaders. At the present time, which can be seen as one of evolution, the personal style and philosophy of the individual overall leader still appears to play a significant role.

Leadership within the teaching schools initiative has not been confined to senior leadership, and there has been a conscious effort to involve staff at various levels. This has provided the opportunity for staff to develop new skills and to work in different contexts. In many cases, middle leaders in teaching schools have been given the chance to work in a range of schools that are very different from their own home institution. These opportunities do come at a cost, and it is important for school leaders to balance this in terms of support and the provision of training and development. However, this type of activity can contribute to middle leaders' own personal professional development and also provide greater opportunities for career progression as we can see from Case example 6C.

Case example 6C

As the principal of a large teaching school in the northwest area of England, quite close to the North Wales border, Gordon describes the aspect of leading such a school that gives him the most satisfaction on a personal level. He said,

> One of our commitments as a Teaching School is to identify and develop future leaders. When I was head of a maintained single school, I had become depressed about how few of my staff, however talented, wanted to go on to principalship or in some cases any form of leadership role at all. They tended to say it was not worth it, either for the money or the work or the responsibility or whatever. I guess they looked at me and decided it wasn't worth it. They just wanted to focus on their teaching and their department. I am really excited now in the teaching school and all the linked schools in the alliance, we make a special effort to identify potential leaders and then give them opportunities to check and develop

that potential. We have now developed a whole range of ways in which
we offer leadership training, at both middle and senior level. Context, as
you know, can be crucial in leadership effectiveness, so it is worth noting
that where an identified future leader is asked to do something in a
particular context and then it does not seem to work, we don't count that
as a failure; instead we learn from it. I have found on a personal level that
these people in fact most of our future leaders seem to be keen to hear
about my failures rather than any successes! Actually, it is true that we
learn so much that way, isn't? I know I do. By sitting down with them and
analysing what happened, we find that they are mostly keen to go on and
try something else. That's the key really, you cannot give up. Fortunately,
in the alliance schools, we can offer that and I know no greater personal
pleasure than seeing some of these people go on to leadership elsewhere
and we are having a lot of success there. I believe I have a responsibility to
provide opportunities for our staff and also a responsibility to the broader
system. This will benefit the school because my staff will be motivated
and purposeful and proactive. Providing leadership opportunities has to
be good for our educational system, and is an important part of school
improvement surely!

In their major evaluation of the teaching school initiative, Gu et al. (2016: 77) have
reported that, 'In all case study teaching school alliances, the expansion of the
teaching school work has created new leadership development and promotion
opportunities across different levels.' However, they also point out that 'talent management and succession planning across the TSA remains the most difficult part of
the job. This requires a change in outlook, perhaps even off culture as, understand-
ably, headteachers are often reluctant to lose their best teachers to other schools'
(ibid: 155). Not every school principal finds they can be as generous as Gordon in
Case example 6C in recognizing the wider needs of the education system and the
potential contribution they can make to address a range of leadership issues outside their school and across the system as a whole. As noted earlier, if standards
in the home school decline, not only is the leader's own situation in jeopardy but
potentially so is the validity of the whole collaborative structure! It is easy to see
how confidence in a 'lead' school would evaporate if its own achievements fell away,
not only within that school but across the alliance as a whole.

However, it is true that a significant aspect of leadership of this type of
initiative has to be an awareness of the broader needs of the education system. Without this, the teaching school initiative is unlikely to be sustainable.
Headteachers have to balance the needs of their own school against the needs of
other schools they are working with. Unless sufficient attention is paid to ensuring continuity of leadership, there is a danger that any impact will be superficial

rather than permanent. Part of the solution has to be ongoing provision of sufficient resources to ensure that future leaders are able as well as prepared to invest
time and energy in working with other schools. Relationships between school
leaders is an important factor in delivering positive outcomes, and clear leadership within schools is also essential to ensure success.

There also has to be clear identification of what the fundamental purpose
of the teaching schools initiative is and how success is measured. At the present time, there is a shortage of data on the impact of the teaching schools on
student outcomes. We have shown in this chapter the benefits to school leaders,
schools and their staff. It is difficult to disagree with the view expressed by Gu
et al. (2016: 190):

> Thus teaching schools and their alliances can make and have made a marked
> difference to the sharing of good practice among schools and to enhancing the
> professional practice of many teachers and school leaders within and beyond
> alliance partnerships. In this sense, the teaching school model has an important
> role in driving forward a school-led 'self-improving' system.

What its future or long-term impact will be is a matter for debate.

Conclusion

Teaching schools are just one example of school collaboration. Many of the
schools participating in this initiative will be involved in a number of other collaborative ventures. It is often difficult to determine the overall impact of an initiative of this type because of the complexity of other policy initiatives that are
operating at the same time. Throughout this book, we have emphasized the positive nature of school-to-school collaboration and the importance for the system
as a whole of schools that work together. The teaching school initiative is a
sophisticated, wide-ranging and more advanced example of collaborative activity that may have the capacity to contribute to a self-improving system. How
far the teaching schools can actually facilitate the creation of a self-improving
system remains to be seen. To do that, the teaching schools will need to become
a long-term model of good practice. Hargreaves (2014) has argued that to create
a 'self-improving school sub-system schools will have to:

- help lower performing schools improve more rapidly;
- embed a commitment to continuous improvement in new forms of professional development for teachers;
- through joint practice development go beyond the better distribution of
  good practice to a more sustained generation of innovative practice;

- strengthen self-evaluation and challenge;
- extend the moral purpose of teachers beyond their own school and its clusters to embrace all members of the school system as a whole' (p. 711).

Given constant changes to policy and during a period of financial austerity, it will be a challenge for schools and their leaders to sustain the developments that have already taken place in the system. However, if the schools and their teachers are committed to this way of working, the initiative will continue to develop.

Summary

This chapter has:

- described the background to the establishment of the teaching schools;
- reflected on the development of the policy;
- identified aspects of good practice in successful teaching school alliances;
- described the role teaching schools can play in school improvement; and
- reflected on the role of leadership in developing successful teaching school alliances.

Recommended reading

Gu, Q., Rea, S., Smethem, L., Dunford, J., Varley, M., and Sammons, P. (2016). *Teaching school evaluation final report*. Nottingham: National College for Teaching and Leadership.

Matthews, P., and Berwick, G. (2013). *Teaching schools: First among equals?* Nottingham: National College for Teaching and Leadership.

Chapter 7
Leadership in Academy Chains: A New Kind of School Linkage

Introduction

In Chapter 5, we considered how a number of school collaborations in England have been structured around the creation of MATs and federations. In this chapter, we develop some of the ideas introduced in that chapter and question the different ways in which these organizations collaborate and the impact on individual school leadership and identity. This chapter also develops an international dimension by considering some aspects of the charter school initiative in the United States. Therefore, this chapter focuses on the ways in which identities are developed and the impact this can have on individual schools and the wider education communities. The role played by the strategic controlling body and the impact this has on individual school leadership and collaboration is also analysed as various education systems continue to fragment.

The chapter, therefore, considers issues such as the extent of the uniformity that may be encouraged or even enforced across a chain or group of schools and how much creativity/individuality is to be found in these circumstances. It therefore:

- considers the context and background of the growth of groups of schools operating under a single governance structure;
- analyses the nature of collaboration and the impact on school leadership of the establishment of groups of schools operating under a single governance structure;

- examines the leadership role in schools that have developed common governance structures; and
- discusses the extent of autonomy available to individual schools within a common organization.

Context and background

As discussed in Chapter 1, a number of countries have seen the development of networks or chains of schools operating under the control of one group or sponsor. In England, this has been primarily through the creation of MATs where individual academy schools or free schools lose their own individual legal identity and become part of a wider grouping under the control of a sponsoring organization that set up a MAT board. The amount of delegation to individual schools tends to differ between individual boards, but the MAT board has ultimate control over all decisions. Given this potential loss of independence, there are a number of possible reasons why schools would consider becoming part of a MAT:

- Shared accountability can lead to better progress and attainment for pupils and help schools meet rising expectations placed on them by national or regional authorities or by local stakeholders, such as parents.
- School leaders and teachers can share thinking and planning in order to spread expertise and tackle challenges cooperatively to produce better solutions.
- Governors and trustees can work more strategically, especially during challenging times when resources are limited.
- School leaders, teachers and other staff can be shared across more than one school, enabling schools to find different solutions to recruitment challenges, to retain staff by providing new opportunities within the group, and to plan succession more effectively.
- Groups of schools can find it easier to recruit and fund specialist expertise (both specialist teachers and specialists in areas such as data analysis, finance, health and safety) and provide richer curricular and extracurricular activities.
- Shared professional development can be more easily arranged, whether led by staff from one of the partner schools or an outside body.
- The economies of scale through group business management and collective purchasing made possible within larger groups can help schools cope better with shrinking budgets (ASCL, 2016a: 3).

Recent proposals by the government in England to increase the number of selective schools have also reaffirmed its commitment to school improvement through the academies programme and MATs:

> These proposals complement our wider approach to school improvement and our drive to build capacity in the system through multi-academy trusts. It remains the Government's ambition that all schools ultimately benefit from the autonomy and freedom to innovate and to meet the needs of their community that academy status brings, and we will support schools to make this transition. Alongside this, there is a need to build capacity in the system and continue to improve the quality of existing schools, both through our work to support academies and spread best practice. (DfE, 2016: 7–8)

The development of MATs in England is, therefore, a central part of the ongoing drive to bring about school improvement and to raise standards for all school students. In the United States, the establishment of charter schools has similar aims:

> Charter public schools are publicly funded, non-sectarian, independently managed schools of choice almost entirely supported by federal and state tax-payer funds. The origin of public charter schools stems from a belief that parents and guardians should be empowered to choose what education program their students may attend and a belief that to reform public education, significant changes had to occur in the way schools are run. (Hays, 2013: 38)

In the United States, there are differences between states, but individual charter schools can join an education management organization (EMO), a charter management organization (CMO) or operate as a stand-alone institution. While both types of organization control a number of schools, EMOs operate on profit basis and CMOs are non–profit-making organizations. There has been a steady increase in the number of charter schools operating as part of either an EMO or a CMO. It has been estimated that between 35 and 40 per cent of charter schools are part of an EMO (Baker and Miron, 2015). Miron and Nelson (2002) outline the changes and perceived outcomes from the introduction of charter schools. Figure 7.1 summarizes the intended process.

In England and the United States, there has been consistent growth in the number of MATs, EMOs and CMOs. For example, 65 per cent of eligible schools in England are currently in MATs. There has been considerable debate about the effectiveness of academy schools and free schools in England and about the performance of charter schools in the United States; see, for example, Beckett (2007) and Epple et al. (2015). However, they have become a significant part of the system and are playing an increasing role in the education of significant numbers of young people. As the number of autonomous schools continues to grow in England and the United States, it is reasonable to assume that there will also be a corresponding growth in schools working together in formal organizations.

Figure 7.1 The charter school concept

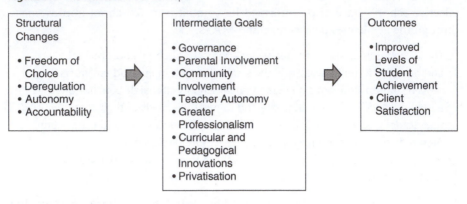

The nature of collaboration

There will be differences within the extent of collaboration in individual MATs, CMOs or EMOs. It is anticipated that there will be formal governance structures in place and that there will be a person with overall leadership responsibilities who has ultimate authority. However, across different groups of schools, there is likely to be considerable variance between the amounts of control exerted by the controlling groups. Whatever the extent of central control, there is a need for clear communication, regular monitoring and identification of responsibilities. The schools may either continue to operate broadly as individual organizations or be tightly controlled from the centre with each school following a tightly-laid-down set of controls. Laura, a head of department in a school that is part of a large MAT in the southeast of England, explained in an interview how the level of control is spread across individual schools:

> Compared to schools and other academies I've worked in before, this is all very tightly controlled. In my last school we had plenty of freedom and we didn't even know we were part of a MAT. Here there is total control on what we and the kids do. We have to do the same topics and have the same lesson plans. Assessment is closely co-ordinated, really it's the same everything across all the schools in the MAT. There are the same discipline rules and uniform rules that are rigorously enforced. Speaking to colleagues in the other schools it's the same set of rules for everyone. It's complete rigidity. Forget spontaneity! We are all part of one big chain.

It is easy to see why this approach might be favoured by many groups and indeed by many teachers. Within a successful school, it is important to establish clarity and common standards. Setting high expectations and establishing a safe learning environment can be significant factors in improving student outcomes (Hays, 2013). However, many teachers, while strongly supporting high expectations and standards, believe that professional teacher autonomy can play a significant part in raising student achievement rather than a 'one size fits all' approach.

Depending on the level of central control, the role of the headteacher is likely to change when a school becomes part of a wider controlling group such as an EMA, EMO or CMO. Some of the broader management requirements that have increasingly taken up senior leadership time may be subsumed by the controlling group, thus freeing the principal or headteacher to focus on curriculum and teaching issues as reported in Case example 7A.

Case example 7A

Dawn has been the principal of a charter school in an urban area of the state of North Carolina for three years. The company, which is a CMO managing many charter schools in several states, took over three failing schools and converted them to charter schools, with a contract to improve their performance to the level of other 'good' state schools within four years. Dawn is confident of this being achieved. She relishes the freedom that she believes she has to focus on what happens in the classroom and raise children's levels of attainment. She explains that, 'The company deals with all marketing, teacher recruitment and all the finance and resources matters. All students wear uniform and pay no tuition fees. We have increased the hours of the day at school by starting earlier and finishing later, and also increased the length of terms so that over a year, children get something like fourteen days per year more teaching and learning. We impose a strict discipline behaviour code and parents have to buy into and they are very supportive. It's become a very safe place for the students and we've created a safe learning environment. If a child is absent over a certain length of time without good reason, the family risks losing its place at the school, so we find parents back us in getting them to school. As a principal, I am free from much of the bureaucracy I used to have to deal with. So now, I can focus on what I became a teacher for –helping these children to learn and achieve better. Most of my job now is about monitoring teachers, trying to inspire them, reviewing their work and that of their students; it's tiring but rewarding as you expect teaching to be! The problem in some places is that the best teachers are lost to the children and the classrooms when they are promoted to being leaders – they spend all their time on administration. Working with the other schools really helps as well. Here, I am able to be in the classrooms, dealing with students and teaching related issues eighty per cent of the time!'

Cravens et al. (2012: 473) have reported on the way in which leadership in American schools, which have been subject to school choice reform, has been influenced by different governance structures: 'Our results suggest that charter management organizations may help reduce the uncertainty charter school principals encounter, thus reducing their need to play boundary-spanning roles and increasing their ability to focus on the technical core of schooling: instructional leadership.'

A similar reduction in the extent of bureaucracy and the potential freeing of headteachers from some of the more mundane administrative tasks and the opportunity to focus increased time and effort on curriculum development was reported in a school that was visited as part of the research for this book. The positive view of the opportunities provided to the new headteacher is described in Case example 7B.

Case example 7B

When a large secondary school of over a thousand students in the north of England became an academy in 2013, the serving headteacher was given early retirement, and a new principal, Neil, was appointed to lead the new academy. The new academy school become part of a large MAT with a number of other academies in different parts of the country. As Neil described it, 'Everything was new – new school name, new uniform, new leader (me!), new board of governors and chances to appoint new staff! It has been a revelation as well as a revolution! We have appointed a whole new leadership team, and a large number of newly qualified teachers. We are able to fund several of them to study for higher degree courses, which of course helps to tie them with us for at least three years. With some of our more local MAT schools we've also developed an MA programme with our local university. We have been able to work with other schools in the MAT and to learn from them. A big bonus, as far as I am concerned is that we have reshaped our curriculum, placing more emphasis on technology and computer skills, which fits in with our sponsor's interests and which the other schools in the MAT had done. I see this as what the nation needs most in the future, and it equips our students for tomorrow's employment world. The parents certainly seem very happy about it all. I make clear to newly appointed people the conditions about union membership and there has been no trouble getting staff! We seem to work well with our primary schools and also with other city secondary ones. The bureaucracy which I hear some leaders complain about is to my mind much better than that I used to have with a local authority which often seemed to request forms to be filled in to give them data which I couldn't see the point of. Exam results so far have been good and are improving. I have now been asked to chair the coordinating regional board of principals for our academy chain so I am starting to be out of the school more. However, this gives excellent leadership training for my deputies and they are all keen to become principals in other academies eventually. As I see it we're gaining in so many different ways.'

The views of Neil, the headteacher in Case example 7B, support many of the original arguments put forward, earlier in the chapter, for the creation of chains of schools working together. However, there is some evidence to suggest that there can be significant differences between chains of schools in terms of achieving the benefits outlined in Case example 7B. Salokangas and Chapman (2014: 376), in their research on governance in chains of academy schools in England, have argued that 'staff involved expressed a general sense of disappointment regarding the lack of chain-wide activities to bring the schools together and create a platform for sharing practice. It became apparent that that chains did not operates as networks of schools. Instead a hub-spoke model, with the sponsor at the centre, prevailed'.

If the sponsor has a clearly articulated ethos and culture, it is less likely that the problems identified above will arise. If the various schools in a group have not got an agreed ethos and culture that has been communicated and shared, then problems are likely to arise. In this type of collaboration, there needs to be common policies, a shared vision, clear guidance on how to deal with stakeholders and an agreed governance structure. How far the commonly agreed policies go should be a matter of agreement across the group of schools. However, it is to be expected that raising achievement levels of students and the provision of better-quality education for all would be at the core of any vision for the group and would be the underpinning for the development of a common culture.

Autonomy or conformity?

Joining a number of schools in a wider formal group will raise a number of key questions relating to autonomy and conformity. Principals and headteachers in a number of countries, especially in developed ones with devolved school management, have increasingly been given greater independence about the way in which they run their schools. Indeed, a major argument in favour of the reforms that have taken place in England and the United States is to enable schools to respond to local needs and encourage innovation by giving schools greater freedom. Joining a larger controlling group may reduce the amount of autonomy available to individual schools (Salokangas and Chapman, 2014).

There are a number of key issues for schools to consider before they potentially give up their autonomy in return for the benefits that can potentially be gained from working as part of a wider group. Assuming there is a choice and there is not forced integration, if a school is considering joining some form of chain or group of schools such as a MAT, EMO or CMO, what general principles can be put in place to ensure a successful collaboration actually takes place? There are a number of areas that a school will have to consider, as described hereunder.

Vision, values and culture

Is there agreement about the vision, values and culture of the organization, and how will it develop over the next few years? The central objective has to be to improve the educational outcomes for young people, but there are a number of ways this can be achieved. For example, will this be achieved through heavily centralized control of all schools, or will individual schools be allowed to develop according to their own local characteristics? How much discussion and debate will be allowed, or is there a 'party line' that has to be followed? How much acknowledgment is there of the different circumstances facing individual schools? Some schools will be happy to accept central control, but for others it may be a major issue. It is surely of vital importance that schools work with others that have similar vision, values and culture.

Size and reach

If an individual school opts to become part of a larger group of schools with the intention of working closely, their physical proximity might be a factor in determining their ability to cooperate. Technology might be able to overcome some issues and enable certain types of communication to take place, but it will be difficult to develop activities such as joint staffing, combined professional development or shared services. Geographical distance might also lead to some schools becoming isolated. Schools located in different parts of the country will also potentially be operating under different socioeconomic conditions. There is likely to be a greater chance of success if the schools are able to work together through a local hub. Many large and national groups or chains have established a regional network of schools to provide a focussed support network, which is grounded in the local community and is responsive to local needs and issues. Many schools can feel better supported working with other schools that share their concerns and are more locally focussed.

Types of school

A key question facing a school is what type of schools do they want to work with as part of a wider group or chain. There is some merit to working with different types of schools, and there could be the potential to share different areas of expertise. Important lessons can be learnt when high-performing schools work with those that are less successful, and there can also be advantages from working with schools from different age phases and in different contexts. However, there is a likelihood that, as part of a group or chain, a school will want to work with some schools that have similar characteristics and are aware of the challenges faced. It is a matter of balance, but one of the potential advantages from joining together with other schools is the opportunity to be creative and to open up new learning possibilities.

Improving standards

Earlier in the chapter, and indeed throughout this book, we suggested that a major factor in the move to encourage schools to work together is the desire to raise standards of student achievement. This will be a prime factor when schools make a decision about which group or chain to become part of as they move away from autonomous operation. Schools will want to work with other schools that are able to offer support and challenge. If a school is joining an existing group or chain, they will need to look closely at the performance profile of existing schools in the group or chain and judge whether it has had a positive impact on raising standards. Factors such as the amount of support available from the central organization, how schools actually work together and the strength of the other schools will all be important factors in determining whether to join an existing group or chain of schools. The role of the MAT, EMO or CMO in developing a strategy for future improvement will also be important to schools. A central strategy that recognizes the different needs of individual schools will be crucial to achieve school improvement and improved standards.

School leadership and governance

Throughout this book, we have considered issues relating to school leadership and governance and school collaboration. Specifically within a formal grouping such as a MAT, EMO or CMO, there are key issues relating to how the organization will operate. There will be issues around central control and the amount of delegation individual schools and leaders are allowed. It is common practice for there to be one person who acts as a chief executive officer (CEO) or executive leader. The day-to-day involvement of this person will differ between groups and chains, and depending on size, they may have some involvement in the daily management of a school, but it is more common for this person to be responsible for the development of strategic policies across all schools. Operational matters, in individual schools, will usually be left to senior staff to deal with. However, the amount of delegation to individual schools will differ between different groups and chains. The relationship between the CEO and other senior leaders within the schools will be a major factor in ensuring successful outcomes. There has to be effective communication within a supportive framework that allows for effective discussion to take place.

Legal and financial

There are a number of legal and financial issues that a school will have to consider before deciding to join a MAT, EMO or CMO. The school will lose autonomy and become part of a larger group controlled by an external organization. It is important that due diligence is applied to a range of financial issues to ensure money is not diverted away from the classroom. In particular, the controlling organization is likely to take a 'top slice' of any funding, and clear arrangements will have to be made about how this will work in practice. It will also be important to identify how much funding will be delegated to individual schools and how much freedom they will have in the way that delegated funding can be used. In return, some services will be provided centrally, and again the school will need to ensure these are appropriate, of sufficient quality and that there is no duplication of provision.

Key questions

Once a school has considered these issues, the key stakeholders will need to formulate answers to a set of key questions:

- How closely aligned is the ethos and culture of the controlling organization and the school?
- Is the school energized and motivated by its vision? Does the school believe they can achieve what they claim?
- What benefits will being part of the controlling organization bring to the school?
- How do these benefits compare to the costs of the other options available?
- Is there a clear distinction between the short and long term?
- How might the school need to change?
- What costs are likely to arise? (Adapted from ASCL, 2016b)

Case example 7C sets out some of the difficulties faced by a school that were attracted by the prospect of additional funding and illustrates a case of a failure to properly consider all of the variables associated with becoming part of a MAT.

Case example 7C

Rosemary is the principal of a primary academy in a borough of a large metropolitan area in the west of England. The primary school became an academy a year ago and she reflects on the changes:

> Neither I nor my staff really wanted to become an academy but the school governors felt there was no choice because of the significant funds being made available for us if we did so. There were some strong individuals on the governing body who strongly believe that academy status is the way forward for every school. We have been trying to several years to get

finance for rebuild and refurbish two blocks of the buildings which have become very run-down and in some places, almost dangerous, I feel. The local authority did not have the money to help us but a sponsor, a national manufacturing company, was offering the funds, supported by government finance, when we converted to being an academy. In fact, the total sum was more than adequate and we are being able to increase our pupil intake next year. That part is good of course, but I still feel uneasy about it. Why? Well, partly, I object to what I see as a privatization of what I see as every child's right to a free state education (You cannot tell me these sponsors want to put money into schools without wanting something back!). Also, I am accountable to so many groups in the academy set up now, and there is increased paper work all the time. I'm not sure how much we have in common with the other schools in the MAT and I don't really buy into the culture that's being developed. It seems very top down, and although my autonomy, in reality, has always been limited, it's got even worse since we changed status. It's clear that the CEO is directing things and she is not especially open to suggestions from me or any of the other school principals. We are becoming increasingly directed from the centre, I wonder how long it'll be before we all have to wear the same school uniform? Two of my best teachers, and closest allies, left to work in non-academy schools and I lost three governors as well who were local people, replaced by nominees of the sponsors. My final worry is that I am a loyal member of a Teachers' Union and a strong believer in public service and I wonder if that is going to cause conflict at some point between me and my so-called bosses! You could describe me as an extremely reluctant convert to this type of arrangement, but financially it made sense for us as a school who needed investment.

Do they make a difference?

We have explored a number of potential benefits from the development of autonomous schools and their willingness to work together under the control of an external organization such as a MAT, EMO and CMO. However, there have been a number of concerns raised about the effectiveness of some groups in England and the United States. For example, Sir Michael Wilshaw, the chief inspector of schools in England and head of Ofsted, who is a strong supporter of academy schools and MATs, wrote a letter to the Secretary of State for Education in early 2016 raising a number of concerns:

As I said in my latest Annual Report, academisation can lead to rapid improvements and I firmly believe that it is right to give more autonomy to the front line. I also want to be clear that there are some excellent MATS that have made remarkable progress in some of the toughest areas of the country. However, it is crucial that all MATS provide robust oversight, challenge and support to ensure that pupils in all their academies receive a good quality of education.

He went on to identify some major concerns:

- poor progress and attainment, particularly at Key Stage 4;
- leaders not doing enough to improve attendance or behaviour;
- inflated views of the quality of teaching and insufficient scrutiny of the impact of teaching on pupils' progress;
- a lack of strategic oversight by the trust of all academies;
- a lack of urgency to tackle weak leadership at senior and middle levels;
- insufficient challenge from governors and trustees who accepted information from senior leaders, without robust interrogation of its accuracy;
- confusion over governance structures, reflected in the lack of clarity around the roles and responsibilities of the central trust and the local governing bodies of constituent academies. This is not helped by some trusts failing to meet the requirement to publish a scheme of delegation (Wilshaw, 2016).

Wilshaw's penultimate comment highlights the expectation that the actual school leaders, such as principals and headteachers, should not expect their authority to be unchallenged. Any 'cosy' relationship between a principal and the governance body that might have existed has to be seen as a thing of the past, and modern leaders in collaborative groupings should see the sponsors as powerful and accountable bodies, just as the principals are accountable to them.

While there are many examples of successful charter schools, a similar variable picture of quality emerges from the United States; see, for example, Baker and Miron (2015); Carpenter and Peak (2013) and Paino et al. (2014). Epple et al. (2015: 56) summarize this up by stating: 'Taken as a whole, the evidence suggests that accounting for differences in population served, charter schools are not, on average, producing student achievement gains any better than traditional public schools.'

Collaboration of this type might not guarantee successful outcomes and, in some instances, might contribute to additional problems. In some cases, collaboration might reduce if there is a strong central controlling body that is laying down policy with little opportunity for reflection or dissent. This aspect of policy is still developing and will require further research. It is a complex area given the number of sponsoring organizations and, in some cases, the lack of transparency. Salokangas and Chapman (2014: 383) have argued that:

> The relationships between multi-academy sponsors and the academies they run are diverse and are explained through a multiplicity of factors, including

the development phases of individual academies as well as the governance and management strategies and practices adopted by sponsors. Therefore schools considering both conversion to academy status and joining an existing chain of academies face a complex task of identifying the most suitable arrangements for their needs. Detailed information regarding these arrangements is couched in the policy and practice of the sponsors and, as such, is not necessarily transparent or available to the general public, making navigation in this market particularly problematic.

Conclusion

It is clear that there is a long way to go before the way ahead for academies in England and charter schools in the United States becomes settled. As this chapter relates, there is considerable diversity within those groupings at present, and probably other changes will occur before there can be confidence about their future. As far as school leaders are concerned, if we recall the experience of Laura quoted earlier in the chapter, it is interesting to note that she had previously taught and led a department in a school in a middle eastern country that, like most in that region, has a highly centralized educational system. She felt that she had had far greater autonomy both as a teacher and a middle leader there than she now has in this particular academy chain! Perhaps, it should not be assumed that devolved educational systems automatically equal more autonomous schools!

The reforms to the wider education system and the increase in the number of autonomous schools such as academies in England and the charter schools in the United States have resulted in a strong growth in the number of schools that are part of a wider formal organization under the control of a sponsoring organization. The amount of central control will differ between individual organizations, but a potential result is an increase in collaboration between the schools that are operating under this system of governance.

Summary

In this chapter we have:

- described the context and background to the growth of groups of schools in England and the United States operating under a common governance structure;
- considered the extent and nature of collaboration and the impact on school leadership;

- discussed the extent of autonomy available to individual schools; and
- identified concerns associated with this policy development.

Recommended reading

Epple, D., Romano, R., and Zimmer, R. (2015). *Charter schools: A survey of research on their characteristics and effectiveness*. Cambridge, MA: National Bureau of Economic Research.

Salokangas, M., and Chapman, C. (2014). Exploring governance in two chains of academy schools: A comparative case study. *Educational Management, Administration and Leadership*, *42*(3), 372–86.

Chapter 8
Executive Leadership: Leading Schools at a Distance

Introduction

Having described a number of different models of school collaborative groupings in Chapters 4–7, examining the kinds of leadership involved, the differences between these and traditional single-school leadership seem clearer. Here, we consider the leadership in those roles – often referred to as executive leadership – that are detached from individual schools in any conventional sense.

This chapter therefore:

- describes the background of executive school leadership in education and what is normally involved in the role;
- examines a range of such leadership roles and their place in system leadership;
- considers the skills, qualities and motivations that executive leaders believe are necessary to be successful in their roles;
- assesses potential drawbacks and disadvantages in the role;
- discusses the collaborations and communications involved with staff and parents;
- considers whether executive leadership can contribute to increased leadership capacity; and
- briefly reflects on executive leadership and its challenges.

Establishment and development of executive leadership in schools

Particularly since the movement towards self-management and increased auton-omy in various developed countries through the 1990s, such as the United States, Australia, Canada, New Zealand and the UK, the pressure on schools to become more like businesses was perhaps inevitable. In essence, the need and ability to manage one's own resources, rather than rely on regional or national bodies to do so, meant that schools were becoming businesses. Equally inevitable perhaps was the increasing use of the language of business – 'performativity', 'workforce re-modelling', and so on. While some of this development can be seen as deplor-able (Ball, 2003; Ozga, 1995) and at risk of drawing schools away from the key purpose of education of the person, it placed demands on leaders in terms of ensuring they considered such crucial issues as a vision for the school, having a strategic overview and, of course, developing their own relationships between the school and external agencies in the communities they served as well as region-ally and nationally, even sometimes internationally. As this aspect of the leader's role became increasingly important, the traditional concept of one person taking responsibility for all activities associated with a school of the future became out-moded. Wood (2002: 13) argued for new models of school leadership that avoided 'the over-reliance on an individual and the over-exposure of one person inherent in the superhead model'. An example from 2001 showed a secondary school in East England experimenting with a new structure. Fox and Evans (2001: 3–4) describe how the deputy became the head and the former head became a 'chief executive'. The head was in full charge of operational matters, aided by four assis-tant heads, and the executive person was enabled to focus on the overall devel-opment and direction of the school, and also on the school's growing external 'dimension', enabling him to 'establish mutually beneficial partnering arrange-ments'. The school leadership structure is indicated in Figure 8.1.

Speculating about the future and using a nautical metaphor, Fox and Evans (2001: 4) envisage an 'executive working with a small flotilla of ships each having their own captain!'

By 2007, in England, the National College for School Leadership, in dis-cussing new models of school leadership that were 'emerging to cope with the demands of modern school leadership' (NCSL, 2007: 10), mentions 'executive headships' among these new models. By 2010, the role of executive leader of schools was being described in Higham (2010) generally as leadership of more than one school. New forms of collaborative groups of schools emerged in England, such as teaching school alliances (TSAs) and school-led and spon-sored multi-academy trusts (MATs) (see Chapters 1, 5 and 6). Lord et al. (2016) reported that there were 620 executive headteachers in England who worked with approximately 970 schools, identifying them as a key part of the school landscape, and they anticipated increasing demand to more than 3,200 by 2022. If Figure 8.1 may be seen as the first stage, the further stages of this rapid

Figure 8.1 Executive leader (stage one)

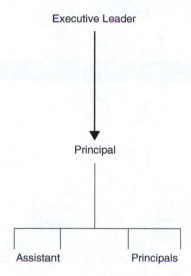

Figure 8.2 Executive leader (stage two)

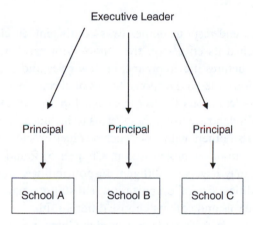

development may be indicated in a simplified form as shown in Figures 8.2 and 8.3.

The stage three in Figure 8.3 might be seen as quite close to the nautical metaphor of the flotilla of ships noted earlier!

Range of executive leader roles in system leadership

Robinson (2011: 74) noted that there was uncertainty in some schools when the executive leader was not present and found that the level and type of allocation

Figure 8.3 Executive leader (stage three)

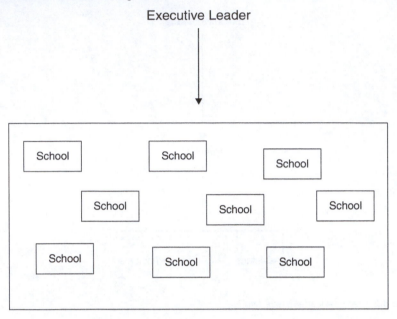

of leadership roles and responsibilities 'was contingent on circumstances and headteachers watched its effects on the school with care'. Lord et al. (2016) noted that new structures inevitably meant new roles and considerable confusion about the various roles and responsibilities of executive headteachers. There may need to be a redefinition of 'executive headship' to 'executive leadership' as school leaders in England are using these terms to include not only headteachers or principals but also others with titles such as chief executive officers (CEOs). The school leaders in our sample (used in Chapter 5) found that leaders with the same job title may have very different responsibilities, and those who have similar responsibilities, size of organization, substantive nature and degree of permanence of the role and context choose different titles.

The school leaders in the sample discussed in Chapter 5 operated in different kinds of collaborative structures, which were at various stages of development. Linda is the executive leader of two primary schools within a mixed-phase diocesan collaborative group, providing close support for the headteachers in the two schools, but as they develop leadership skills, she is able to step back and become more advisory and strategic. Linda is involved in the monitoring and evaluation processes and manages the performance of headteachers in the collaborative group where she is accountable overall for the success of both schools.

Martin is the executive principal of a federation of two schools where there are no longer individual school principals. He relies on his five vice principals for micro-management and is keen to lead and develop them. Mike leads a three-school cross-phase federation and was styled as an executive headteacher of the three schools but CEO of the trust. Brian (see Case example 8A) is the executive principal of a group of three schools.

Case example 8A

Brian was originally employed by the trust to lead a failing school, and after successfully raising it to being 'outstanding', according to inspectors, he was invited to be the executive principal of two other vulnerable schools. He sees his role is to develop the inexperienced principals in the three schools, building cohesion across them and having an overview of the federation. In his words,

> My role is to make sure that principals understand their role and to be a buffer, taking away some of the escalating parental complaints or the overarching educational or LA issues. I want them to focus on the school improvement and then the strategic bit is something I'll take off the pressure for them. I think too well they need to have experience of the strategic aspect so it's a bit of a balancing act. Some of the capital stuff I do, like the pupil numbers and keeping them up to date with policy such as safeguarding or other things that have changed, and also keeping them up to date with the Trust and filter what's important to them and to us.

The principals in each school make individual decisions, but Brian makes decisions that affect the overall group and links directly with the regional director and wider trust board. The role of the executive leader here is subject to accountability to a regional director, but Brian values the high level of earned autonomy granted to him and sees it as a strength of the particular organization. He does not, however, believe he has a high degree of influence within the trust, although some other principals do.

Brian says that his way of working depends on the strengths, vulnerabilities and needs of the organization, which will change as needed. An aspect of the role that is important to him personally is accessibility and visibility to the children and wider community.

Nigel is the CEO of a seven-school cross-phase group. His predecessor was styled as an executive headteacher with headteachers in each of the schools. Now, however, due to the size and complexity of the organization and its wide external links, Nigel is styled as a CEO. Lynne was CEO of a cross-phase group of five schools, including one secondary school (see Case example 5B). 'I'm not directly involved with any school and the role is entirely strategic. Having said that, I am still called on to step in sometimes and it's usually a human resources issue.' Thus, a range of titles exist, probably depending on the size and complexity of the collaborative group – and to some extent the wishes of the individual and their governance boards.

Similarly to the findings of Higham (2010) and Chapman et al. (2011), all the leaders originally started as executive leaders through supporting improvement in another school. As our examples show, some of the other schools in the grouping retained their individual headteachers/principals – others did not. It is unclear as yet whether the use of the role of a CEO for some forms of executive leadership means that another tier of leadership is developing. Executive headship in some cases is possibly similar to traditional headship, but stretched over more schools, with a more overall strategic role being an important aspect of that leadership. The role of a CEO, however, although we draw on a limited sample, may be becoming different and more complex and almost completely strategic.

What seems to be clear is that those people holding the more detached role of one with a strategic overview of the whole group of schools and accountable for their overall performance are akin to someone holding the role of a CEO. Clearly, some individual leaders find it hard to adopt this role and become completely detached from the schools' operational leadership, but this depends on the person, not the role. Wendy, for example, sees herself as a 'shared' headteacher and refuses to accept any title as 'executive'. Whether this particular example relates to the rural nature of her federation is a matter of speculation.

This wider role, more detached and strategic, also raises the question as to whether people holding such an overall leadership role need to have been qualified teachers. If there is no expectation that a CEO as such would be directly involved in leading the schools, can the skills required for effectiveness be found and developed in contexts such as business or industry? The CEOs in the sample interviewed believed they had to have been teachers first, and the following quote is typical:

> I really do believe that CEOs need to have been teachers. My reason for that is the empathy you bring. It's an understanding of the role of a headteacher and more importantly what the role of a teacher is and those demands are. – Nigel

This viewpoint is understandable, is almost certainly widely held throughout the teaching profession, and it also links with Wendy's feeling of personal commitment to 'her' schools.

The issue as to whether a non-educationalist can be an executive leader of a collaborative group of schools is debated further in Chapter 11.

Executive leaders of schools, in their more detached roles and with a remit to take a wider and more strategic view of the place of their own group of schools in the wider context, are obviously ideally situated to make a contribution to that wider landscape. They can gain huge benefits for their own schools but also make observations on and offer developments to the whole system of schooling. Case example 8B includes some thoughts on this.

Case example 8B

John is an executive principal of a group of four schools in the northwest of England, having previously been the headteacher of one of the individual schools concerned. His role is entirely strategic, and he has little or nothing to do with the operation of any of the schools in the group, except when there is some kind of crisis. Even then, he points out that the first point of call for help would be another school's leader within the group, before the issue might come to him if unresolved. John's focus on the strategic aspects of school leadership has enabled him, he says, to gain a 'hugely more meaningful insight into the context within which all schools sit'. He says that it is not all 'edifying'! For John, so many decisions affecting the way schools are required to operate are based on political motivations and self-interest that 'I have become more cynical about it all. Perhaps I was naïve before!' John believes he understands the wider context for school leadership much more now and is in a powerful position to advise his own group school leaders as to the best courses for them. Despite his scepticism about motives and politics, John believes he can achieve the best for the pupils in the group's schools now – and 'this is after all what I became a teacher for'.

Some of the school leaders in our sample have been involved in leadership for school improvement beyond their own organization as system leaders (see Chapter 2). This was either because it was part of a system leadership role they wished to, or were expected to undertake as part of their wider role within a collaborative group. Nigel, for example, is involved in a variety of external school support.

> For the last twelve months I've probably done the equivalent of about a day a week and most of it in the region. – Nigel

Both Nigel and Lynne have other leaders with key roles working outside their own group to support other schools. Mike works as an associate for the school improvement provider contracted by his LA. Martin works as a system leader outside his group (see Case example 8C). Wendy is an LLE and works as a coach across other schools.

Coldron et al. (2014) argue that being able to access important information and being well networked to gain information about national policy are advantages in a competitive environment. School leaders were well placed to receive information because of their work with other organizations. The executive leaders were all seen as exceptionally successful networkers, because of the much wider environments within which they operated.

> We have international links – we have links everywhere! – Martin

Thus, executive leaders bring not only awareness and insights to those running their individual schools within a group but also have a commitment to the 'greater good' of the whole school system.

Skills, qualities and motivations of successful executive leaders

While the school leaders in this study had very different personalities, they had many characteristics, skills and motivations in common, which resonate both with effective traditional school leadership (Leithwood et al., 2006), and the particular skills of executive leadership identified by NCTL (2010a), Higham (2010) and Lord et al. (2016). It also has to be acknowledged that currently literature is 'particularly weak at addressing the skills needed to be a competent executive headteacher' (Fellows, 2016: 6)

Skills

Based on Lord et al. (2016) and our own research, we can suggest that the following skills may be identified as essential for effective executive leadership:

- Strategic thinking – managing change with an understanding of contextual leadership;
- ensuring a relentless focus on school improvement and outcomes;
- highly developed interpersonal skills, including communication skills;
- resilience; and
- being entrepreneurial.

Clearly, such skills can and have been identified as features of effective leadership in most school contexts; thus questions for consideration are whether executive leadership requires a higher level of such skills (and whether some are more important and/or essential than others). Sarah, one of the executive leaders interviewed, succinctly expressed the difference in her eyes as simply being 'more things to more people'.

Strategic thinking and managing change

Understanding 'contingent leadership' (Leithwood et al., 2006) and 'political awareness' (Hummerstone, 2012) and being able to recognize and seize opportunities are characteristics of effective leaders who manage in a rapidly changing policy environment (Robinson, 2012). Managing change lies at the heart of the success of executive leaders whether they were permanently or temporarily leading any kind of collaborative grouping. They recognized the need to understand the style of leadership needed for success in their specific context.

> The individuality of the schools means I have a different style. In the one school I am absolutely a headmistress while in the other I'm 'chuck'. – Wendy

To manage change effectively required them to be strategic thinkers. Lord et al. (2016) argued that executive leaders needed 'higher levels of strategic thinking', and among aspects of strategic leadership thinking, noted by Middlewood (1998: 8), were 'identifying opportunities' and 'constantly examining the external environment'. Through these, the leader can encourage the right kind of change to bring about those new things appropriate to the envisaged new context. Our interviewees agreed.

They were outward-looking and constantly thinking about how the organization, their role and staff might change to shape the future. Increasingly, CEOs and leaders of larger organizations had to understand how to be influential leaders while spending decreasing amounts of time in the schools.

Although, as Sarah noted, leaders were 'putting in all those checking ways of ensuring that people are doing the job', all the leaders interviewed were very keen to stress that distributing leadership to staff was overall a good thing. In supporting other staff to lead in their absence or due to the increased scale of the organization, executive leaders were able to offer staff opportunities and leadership experiences they might otherwise not have had (see Chapter 5).

There is international evidence (Piot and Kelchermans, 2016) that the interests of principals in federations relates mainly to ensuring the success of their organization. All the school leaders showed a single-minded determination to ensure this outcome. Part of ensuring success was to try to understand their role and its impact.

> Many federations go wrong because they haven't thrashed out from the beginning what the role and protocols of the exec head should be. – Sarah
> You have to understand the difference in roles between executive and single headship. You aren't here to lead everything in the school and you might model leadership but your success as an executive head is the leadership and the leaders that you enable or produce. – Linda

It was recognized that leaders needed to be fair to all staff, especially as the organization expanded, and they had to spend more time in other schools.

> A coach described it with an analogy that it's like, 'Martin you were having an affair and now not only are you having an affair but you've moved in with your mistresses!' – Martin

The importance of understanding the impact the change to executive leadership will have on themselves and their leadership style was highlighted.

> For me it's about understanding my own desire to control and being able to recognize that something isn't what I wanted or needed to do but it will be ok. – Sarah

While four executive leaders were open to change, and one leader adamant their federation would not grow, three others were actively seeking growth. Typically:

> I said to the Chair that if it grows we may look at six to eight [schools] … We have to look at the structures we can put in place. – Mike

Relentless focus on school improvement and outcomes

All worked to ensure successful outcomes for pupils especially in tests and examinations. They may not have been operationally involved in leading curriculum or monitoring the quality of teaching, but they had systems in place to inform them of the quality of learning in their schools. Typically, Linda noted that executive leaders needed 'sound knowledge and understanding of educational pedagogy and of leadership'.

Any underperformance in one school had to be eradicated so it was a good experience for all children irrespective of which school they attended.

> There are going to be children who are underperforming and if I can pick which school it's likely to be, then that's wrong because it should be the same for all our children in any school. – Brian

Good interpersonal skills

Motivating others was noted as more challenging across a range of organizations. The influence of executive leaders has to be practised through relationships and interaction with staff as they increasingly lead at a distance from their schools with the consequent need to be an 'absent presence'.

> You have to accept that if you were there in one school all the time, something you don't like wouldn't have happened. – Sarah
> You have to be open and people have to want to listen to you because you've only got them once every three weeks. – Mike

Professionalism in managing relationships was a recurring theme. Typically:

> Relationships have to be professional and an understanding that there will be clashes along the way but any issues have to be worked out in a professional way and not get personal. – Linda

Robinson (2012) found that, although school leaders realized that 'emotional intelligence' (Goldman, 1996) may allow them to motivate staff due to an understanding of the culture or climate in schools, it does not mean that they will necessarily exercise it. Nevertheless, all leaders noted the importance of inspiring staff to lead according to the vision of the schools' leadership:

> I hate the term 'manipulative' leadership because it sounds like bullying but if you think of it positively, it's people who can intentionally influence to get the best out of people … it's getting them to see that they have a lot of offer and to encourage them. – Nigel

Resilience

All leaders felt under pressure to perform, although it affected them personally in terms of stress in different ways and to varying degrees. They were aware that executive leadership involving vulnerable schools brought risk:

> I can honestly say I don't ever fret or worry. I don't think I worry for more than about 15 minutes and I'm not keep awake at night. – Sarah
>
> Resilience is essential to get through it. It's quite lonely and when people say to me I don't know how you do your job, I think 'No, I don't know how myself, you just get through it'. – Mike
>
> I have had to be incredibly resilient particularly initially with the unions and the local politician who was so anti. We got the whole gamut of nasty publicity and personal attacks for a while. – Lynne

Entrepreneurial

Developing partnerships, including those that could bring in resources or financial income, was important to all if they were involved in system leadership. While part of their wider role was to contribute to the whole system, they did not miss opportunities to gain resources for their schools, to enlarge budgets to benefit the children in their schools. They also saw generating income as allowing them to retain and recruit staff. Therefore, while trying to be as altruistic as reasonable, these leaders would usually charge for work undertaken (see Chapter 5).

Characteristics

These related to leaders being:

- trustworthy
- courageous and
- credible.

Trustworthiness

This was cited by all as an essential characteristic for executive leaders especially when they often are not there to immediately put right any misunderstandings or errors.

It's like any leadership in that you need to be trustworthy and have credibility and it's still like headship [in a school] and they [the staff] have to believe that you are genuine. – Linda

Courage

Leaders noted that it was important for them to know what they believed in and have the courage and confidence to fight for it:

If you always stand up for what you believe in, then your values never change and that's how you lead the school. – Nigel
You have to be courageous and use your voice as you are fighting for survival with small rural primary schools all the time. – Wendy

Credibility

For executive leaders, much of any credibility for system leadership or for working across multiple schools came from past experience and reputation.

I think it's helped that I led an outstanding school before, so I had a reputation for leadership in place before I started. As the year has gone on, credibility has increased and everyone does acknowledge that I'm there for the children and not the status and power. – Linda

Much of the above is applicable to traditional headship, but Sarah typifies views as to how executive leadership differs:

I think characteristics are broadly the same as headship but perhaps more magnified in executive leadership as you are more things to more people.

Motivation

Personal values

All agreed that they were motivated by a love of the job.

If you didn't love it and have a passion for children to succeed, you wouldn't do this job. – Sarah

Chapman et al. (2011) noted that extending the role of heads when they worked externally was often accompanied by changes in the 'perception' of leadership and the leadership for all the children in a group of schools. Hargreaves (2008)

found a similar moral purpose in leaders who led across schools in Finland. In this research, there were similar examples of leading ethically with moral purpose.

Typical responses

If you get a school on the other end of the phone that has just gone into a [failing] category and has a problem with maths and wants help but has no money then you are not going to say no to them . . . it's not about the money, but more about all young people being entitled to have the best education they can. – Nigel

My dad was a head and his job was to rescue run-down vulnerable schools. It was a fascinating perspective as a child to witness the real poverty that existed. It's made me ethical and driven and prepared to be a similar model. – Wendy

Professional challenge

Leaders viewed executive leadership as an opportunity, and this 'buzz of professional challenge' was a key motivation, particularly for those leaders undertaking external roles (Robinson, 2012).

I have to challenge myself. When I stop feeling that challenge, then it's time to go and do something else. – Mike

I had taken the other school to being classed as 'outstanding' and my motivation then was that, while it was a joyous situation to be in, it was sad in a way because it was mission accomplished. Now as an executive head I have been challenged to lead in a different way. –Linda

Potential drawbacks and disadvantages in the role of executive leader

Robinson (2011) noted that in some schools there was uncertainty over who was leading the school when the executive leader was absent or unavailable, especially for a lengthy period. Despite the best efforts of school leaders, as they left to take on an executive leadership role, the disruption seemed to unsettle some staff who could not perhaps acknowledge the new context as their own daily seemed relatively unchanged. Perhaps they saw the headteacher's departure to the new role as simply for ambition and as an astute career move.

Some of the leaders interviewed expressed regret that they had to lose the contact with children and young people because their executive role meant they worked 'at a distance' from the school's daily work. They had virtually no opportunity to build relationships with them or their families. Parents inevitably had loyalties to a particular school in the group, the one their children attended, and could not be expected to see the wider picture of the whole federation or chain. Executive leaders recognized the importance of parents and their support and links with the schools, but were restricted mainly to relationships with any parents through school governing bodies. Similarly, they missed the way relationships could be built with school staff, especially helping new staff to be appointed and developed. One of them, Mike, said that he hoped to do that kind of relationship building again before he finally retired, by returning to the leadership of a single school, although this was not an ambition shared by others. All interviewees made the point that such things had been the reasons why they entered the teaching profession in the first place and, therefore, were bound to miss them in a quite different role.

Some executive leaders were well aware that their role, involving as it does a much greater sphere of accountability and responsibility (and a higher salary!), could be seen by others as to do with power and driven by desire for 'empire building'. Mike said, 'The danger is that it CAN get too big and maybe people can get too big for their boots?' Certainly, such leaders exert a good deal of influence, especially in the region where the group was located, as recognized by Coldron et al. (2014). There is a growing body of research and literature that suggests that school leaders who effectively build sustainable cultures for the future are in fact most likely to be selfless, having a quiet determination, patience and a compelling modesty. As Middlewood and Abbott (2017: 141) suggest, such leaders 'are never the flag-waving, loudly charismatic types who may for example bring about a change overnight'.

The removal of executive school leaders from some of the actual leadership and management processes of a school (see Bush and Middlewood, 2013) can have its dangers. Particularly, this may be true of recruitment and selection of school staff. If, as Collins (2006: 3) suggests, the most important part of building a successful organization for the future is 'Getting the right people on the bus', then the leader not being involved in finding these people seems illogical. On the other hand, if leadership capacity is to be increased, perhaps this is precisely the area in which new and potential leaders need to lead. At this interim stage, it may be why the majority of the interviewed executive leaders came back to school(s) to help with staff selection, especially of senior staff. Others had reached the stage of leaving all recruitment and selection to the individual operational leader, presumably confident that the agreed vision for the schools was so well established that the actual process of choosing the right people to make it happen could be left to others.

Collaboration and communication with staff and parents

There was a consensus that there were overall benefits for the community in the growth of their organization and their own change of role. While some leaders operate with a high degree of control, they believe they are optimizing benefits for their communities as well as for themselves. Links with key stakeholders remain crucial.

Staff

Much of the benefits for staff lay in the opportunities they had for advancement within their own schools in stepping up in the absence of the executive. There were substantive roles generated as a result of another tier of leadership being introduced and experience gained across the organization leading to improvements in their own pedagogical understanding and practice (see Chapter 5). As noted earlier, it was not possible for executive leaders who were totally detached and strategic to build close relationships with colleagues in any school. However, regular communication with the staff as a whole was absolutely essential, and it is important to strike a balance between adding to the regular information staff received and making sure they were up-to-date with developments across the schools' group. The other key issue here was collaborating closely with the individual leader of the school to decide from whom certain information should come. Some of the interviewees saw this as an advantage that the extra level of detachment from daily interaction of executive leaders meant that they could be used as a broker on occasions of complaint. As Linda suggested, 'I can offset some of the emotion because I am not the actual head on the spot.' It is also possible that on occasions, the operational leader can 'pass the buck' to the executive overall leader of the group.

Parents

All accepted that ensuring that parents were satisfied with the organization (i.e. school grouping) overall was part of their accountability, which they saw as a benefit for parents. The amount of interaction, however, depended on the nature of the role of the executive leader and the level of operational responsibility, if any. Primary leaders tended to have the most frequent interaction. Typically:

> We have to manage our families extremely well because as primaries they expect to have access to us whatever and so we have to be very clear about managing their expectations. – Sarah

At the beginning of the changes, Martin noted that it was important that parents understood and were communicated with effectively because, despite best efforts,

> In both schools initially, parents have found it difficult to know who to see.

Those executive leaders who were wholly detached spoke about parental interaction mainly in terms of governance

> You do need parents' involvement. We suggest using the parent clinics and could use that to find out what the parents think and want and get their views and focus through that because the governors' board needs to be focussed more strategically. – Mike

The executive leaders all recognized the importance of communicating with parents as to how and why the structure of the organization and their role developed.

> We've explained to our families that we've set up a clear and effective structure and it will be keeping the strong teachers in school. If we didn't have these opportunities then I say that I would be gone and so would my two deputies. The price they pay for that is that we aren't here all of the time everyday but they do get us at least some of the time and my families understand that and know what the climate is like out there and that we can't get good people easily. – Sarah

As noted, parents identified with a particular school, and this also led to a sense of loyalty to which the majority in the sample referred. It affected three of the primaries who wanted to offer the children an experience in any school in the overall grouping that best suited the individual children's needs but who also recognized that parents might not understand the whole organization's approach in relation to the daily teaching of their children

> Parents identify with their school. But we're asking whether we can move children across sites around the federation to get the best provision for them? Who makes such decisions? – Brian

When your child enters a particular school, and does not do well, what is the scope for movement within and across a collaborative group? Communication between the parties concerned clearly remains the crucial element in resolving individual cases, but are there principles to be established here?

Occasionally, special and specific events were organized on behalf of the whole group, but generally, schools were shown to be very individual and with varying degrees of parental interaction.

> In one school there are strong parental relationships but in this school we struggle to get parents through the door. What works well is recognizing early on that you can't impose one model of a school on to the other. It's about what can be shared and what needs to be individual. – Martin

This ability to recognize differences between individual schools within the group is seen as crucial and a challenge for leaders of collaborative groups. The reference here is to differences between schools on levels and quality of parental involvement, but the principle is an important one and is discussed further in Chapter 9 and to some extent in Chapter 10.

Building increased leadership capacity

The literature has recognized executive leadership as a 'powerful lever for change' when used to 'mobilise and release leadership energy between and across schools' (Harris and Abbott, 2006). The success of executive leaders in building capacity in multiple organizations was perceived as an advantage of federations and MATs, together with distributing leadership to staff and creating new roles (see Chapter 5).

It was a specific role for those who had federated as a 'performance federation' (Chapman, 2011), brokered and developed locally by a school with strong internal capacity to support (Higham, 2010).

> I agreed to support the leadership in the first instance in late July. I went in September to fact find and on the first day we had the Ofsted call. The inspection gave the school a Requires Improvement (RI) grading. – Brian

Working with the principal of the RI school, Brian and the principal successfully improved it so that a subsequent school inspection graded the school as 'good'. For Linda and Sarah, each had a role specifically to coach and build the leadership capacity within a MAT.

There is even a risk of actually reducing leadership capacity if the use of executive leaders to support other schools stretches that capacity too far; this may happen if a sponsor is encouraged or tempted to take on too many vulnerable schools, for example:

> What worries me is that some sponsors have so many struggling or vulnerable schools that they don't have the capacity overall to move them on. – Linda

Overall, the interviewees felt that, if managed well, leading across many schools was believed to add to leadership capacity and that it would be to the advantage of all schools to collaborate in some way especially as part of a strong alliance or federation.

> I think in terms of a maturity model [for the system] while what it looks like keeps changing . . . I think you are 'there' when every school is linked in to one or more group of schools. – Nigel

It would make it easier to stretch leadership across those schools that found it difficult to recruit.

> If a head has a good background and capacity to pick up another school, either temporarily or permanently, then that's a better option than going out and getting four applicants from people who are speculative in their application for headteacher. – Mike

All of the organizations used some form of system leadership to build capacity, and the advantages gained from doing so, articulated in this chapter and others, are evidence that the whole is more than the sum of its parts. A caveat, however, is in the apparent lack of succession planning for future executives. It was believed that people with the complex knowledge and skills needed for the job might be difficult to find:

> There isn't a big field of people to replace CEOs like me. Most of the people who are already doing it are thinking about a few years more and then retiring. I'm not sure we [the education system] have built up enough capacity in the layer of people underneath that level . . . There isn't a properly thought through programme for growing executive headship. – Lynne

The extent to which this is based on the fact that, at this stage of collaborative school groupings, leaders tend to be designing their own roles so that they make the most of their own particular personal abilities and qualities for the benefit of the schools is, of course, unclear. It is after all a human trait, however modest one might be, to think that there are not many who can do the job like ourselves! The real question is in fact whether they really need to be 'like us' to be equally successful!

While executive headship has been successful in building leadership capacity, it is not by itself a silver bullet of reform and perhaps many of the elements identified in the characteristics of executive leaders earlier, and a planned and coordinated approach to collaboration between them need to be in place for success.

Reflections on leadership

- If a group of collaborative schools establishes a pathway that shows someone can become a vice principal, then a principal, and then an executive or a director, they may be building expectations that are difficult to maintain. This is because the only way an organization can do that is through continual growth, which obviously cannot be guaranteed.
- Managing leadership 'at a distance' is an issue for those leaders who still have some responsibility for an individual school or schools.

- Determining the balance between strategic and operational practice was a particular issue in times of growth and organizational change.
- Leaders motivating staff through sharing opportunities and offering experiences helped them to appreciate the benefits of the executive role of the headteacher.
- The buzz of professional challenge, if not managed carefully, could encourage executive leaders to take on too much, without realizing the risks to their organizations, which include those 'taking their eye off the ball'.
- Tension between autonomy and control can exist in the leader's relationship with staff with shared leadership responsibilities.
- Ongoing high-quality professional development for executive leaders was either difficult to access, or it was ineffective because of the trainers' lack of understanding of the rapidly changing role of executive leaders.
- Effective executive leaders are contingent leaders who can adapt leadership to suit changing circumstances.

Summary

This chapter has:

- described the beginning and development of executive leadership in schools;
- examined a range of executive leadership roles and the reasons they were established;
- considered the skills, qualities and motivations that executive leaders believe are necessary to be successful in their roles;
- considered some of the drawbacks and disadvantages in the role;
- discussed the collaboration and communication needed with staff and parents;
- considered if and how executive leadership brings about increased leadership capacity; and
- briefly reflected on executive leadership and some of its challenges.

Recommended reading

Davies, B. (2006). *Leading the strategically focused school*. London: Paul Chapman. This book gives an excellent view of the importance of school leaders ensuring that a strategic approach is given to all aspects of their work. It gives much sound practical guidance.

Lord, P., Wespieser, K., Harland, J., Fellows, T., and Theobald, K. (2016). *Executive headteachers: What's in a name? A full report of the findings.* Slough, Birmingham, and London: NFER, NGA, and TFLT. This report is based on in-depth research into the emerging roles of executive school leaders.

Part Three

Implications for School Leadership

In this section, we try to summarize some of the issues and implications for the future of school leadership, after the research into five different kinds of examples of collaborative school leadership. In Chapter 9, we try to draw together some of the features that, based on our research, we feel perhaps characterize what is effective in this kind of school leadership. In Chapter 10, in a more speculative and perhaps idealistic way, we anticipate some of the possibilities when these implications have been taken beyond the immediate future. Then, in Chapter 11, we consider some of the practicalities that need to be addressed and the actions that may need to be adopted and adapted to ensure that collaborative leadership becomes as effective as possible.

Chapter 9
Effectiveness in Collaborative School Leadership

Introduction

Having described and discussed the research carried out in various kinds of school collaborative groupings, with an emphasis on the leadership involved, we here try to draw these separate pieces of research together and examine whether there are common features that can be discerned. This chapter therefore:

- makes some general observations on the models of collaborative leadership;

- notes briefly some factors found that are common to effectiveness in most kinds of school leadership;

- presents some aspects of effectiveness that seem especially crucial in collaborative school leadership;

- discusses some of the challenges that seem especially pertinent to collaborative school leaders; and

- refers to some conditions identified as essential to ensuring successful collaborative leadership.

Overall

In a period of rapidly changing organizational structures in several educational systems, there are clearly a number of different models within which forms of collaborative school leadership occur. These were outlined in Chapter 1, and then in the chapters of Part II of this book, we described the issues, particularly those related to leadership, that we identified in our research into some of these models. These models ranged from simply pairing the leaders of two schools together to a context where a leader is separate from a whole group of schools that he or she is in charge of. It would be foolish to expect that the kind of leadership would be the same for each of these models, or indeed perhaps for any two of them. After all, we know that school leadership is highly contextualized anyway, even for single schools. Our research, which involved talking with a large number of principals and headteachers, both at primary and secondary level, and also a smaller number of special school leaders, revealed a number of leadership characteristics that recurred regularly. While the personality and character of the individual person in the role of school leader differed of course, these characteristics became clearer. Unsurprisingly, many of them corresponded to those identified in much other leadership research carried out in a variety of contexts by other researchers and academics. We have decided, therefore, that it would be helpful to note a few of the more significant of these firstly – and we stress that they are only a few of the many identified in the leadership literature! Thus, they were common to all the leaders in collaborative schools, but not necessarily those that we found were the most significant for success in leading collaboratively. Our second list, therefore, records what we found those to be.

Features common to effective school leadership

Our research indicated that the following features played their part in effective collaborative school leadership, in the sense that they were found to be common to all the individual leaders we visited and interviewed.

Developing a vision

All effective collaborative school leaders had a clear vision of what the features of the collaborative group would be in the future. They were clear that it would have a strong moral purpose and focused on the learning of all those involved. This is what made the whole enterprise worthwhile and could be used to inspire them and all those who worked in the schools. Thus, certain key values remained at the heart of such visions, underpinning the culture of the organization. Such values included honesty and integrity, equity, loyalty, respect for inclusion and diversity, striving for the highest possible attainment, social justice, and a belief in the innate worth of each individual. Such values are likely to be agreed and proposed in many, if not most, debates about educational leadership, but that is no reason for not mentioning them here as things that collaborative leaders felt strongly about. Above all, underpinning any vision in education was a strong moral purpose, that of acting in the best interests of the children and young people concerned.

What collaborative leaders could not envisage in their visions for the future was any clear idea of the form or structure of the schools' grouping in the future. Some believed there would probably be many and various forms and some of those felt this was a positive notion because of the need to avoid uniformity. On the other hand, some feared that a lack of a 'true model' of a collaborative structure would run the risk of continuing the problem of a division between the advantaged and the disadvantaged in society – 'The gap will stay wide if we do not have a clear and definite model to which all forms of collaboration adhere,' according to one school leader. Others felt that the diversity would disappear when it was recognized which model eventually was seen as most effective in raising attainment levels. The biggest concern noted by every single school leader was the 'interference' of political parties and governments that were seeking a 'quick-fix'. As another principal noted, 'Governments lose faith so quickly when improvement is not immediately apparent!' Another pointed out that it was 'precisely in the field of educational structures that national governments do think they know best and are constantly proposing change!' Therefore, the commitment to a vision for collaborative school leaders was focused positively on the values noted earlier, irrespective of the precise form of the collaborative structure.

Commitment to high-quality teaching and learning

Obviously, this feature will be present in any leader's list of requirements for effectiveness. It also involves, therefore, a strong concern for various stages and processes of people management within the schools. Thus, careful recruitment and selection processes in trying to ensure the use of the most capable staff, and attention paid to staff induction into the specifics of not just the individual school but the collaborative group of schools, were both evident. Rigorous appraisal procedures played a very important role in all the schools and groups concerned, not just of teachers but of all those employed there. CPD was seen as crucial, especially that which was carefully based on identified needs and specific to the school and/or the collaborative group.

Factors especially relevant to collaborative leadership

Not all of the following factors are unique to anyone involved in collaborative leadership, but they have been found from our research to be especially significant for being effective in that. Certainly, it is difficult to envisage someone succeeding in the role without possessing at least most of them.

Ability to see 'the big picture'

This strategic aspect of school leadership, while important to any effective school principal or headteacher, is fundamental for success to anyone in a leadership role involving two or more schools. It is absolutely essential that collaborative leaders are able to look beyond the daily and regular operations of the schools and take a broader view across all the schools involved, seeing the overall sense of direction towards some kind of common goals, and the developing culture of the group as a whole. Strategic leadership involves having a longer-term view, and therefore, the ability to place any new set of requirements (national policy changes, for example) in the context of that longer-term plan or vision is crucial. This is not to suggest that the path ahead is fixed – far from it! Strategic leaders are constantly examining the external environment to discern new mega-trends (Caldwell and Spinks, 1992) and distinguishing them from new 'fads' or 'band-wagons'. They are alert to potential dangers, therefore, and more importantly to identifying opportunities that would be to the group's advantage and enhance the learning of those involved.

Such environmental scanning, as it is known, needs to encompass aspects that are not only local or regional, but national and even international. At a local or regional level, strategic leaders will note population and demographic develop-ments as to how these are likely to influence schools in the future; at a national level, the ideology of a new government may presage a totally new emphasis in educational priorities, while, internationally, technological initiatives or migra-tion trends may be likely to have a considerable impact on the school group's ideas for the years ahead. It is well known that in any organization, seeing the link between any kind of strategic planning and the reality of daily operational work is a difficulty for staff in those organizations (West-Burnham, 1995). It is crucial, therefore, that collaborative school leaders have their perspectives that range across all the schools involved and beyond them to the education system and ideally the place of that system within the wider educational world.

One of the reasons why this strategic role is so important in collaborative groups is that often staff working in individual schools need a reference point to place their hard work in a wider context; this is best provided by someone able to stand outside the 'hurly burly' of their daily life. When staff question why some-thing is necessary to be done, sometimes the answer can only be provided by some-one with that external perspective on the future of the schools and their learners.

An important element of strategic thinking is the ability and willingness to practice being reflective. In the sometimes frantic pressures of operational life in busy schools, it is essential for leaders to be able to 'renew themselves by taking time out to think, to learn and relax' (Hill, 2006: 79). Starratt (2003: 2–3) refers to this as being able to 'rise above the daily managerial processes and crises to gain different perspectives'. These perspectives critically involve looking back as well as looking forward so that 'wise risks' (ibid) can be taken to avoid mistakes being repeated in the future.

It should also be noted, however, that detachment to enable a strategic overview should never mean isolation! If a strategic leader is too distant, the staff are not likely to take much notice of them when they have something to say. Goldstein (1998: 116) pointed out how dangerous it was for any leader or top management to isolate itself from the 'front line', describing it as not only unhealthy but also ultimately unproductive.

Achieving sustainability

Whatever definition of sustainability is accepted, there will certainly be an element of 'doing no harm to others' within it. For leaders who operate outside of or across a group of schools, it is clear that this has to be an important ingredient in their approach and their philosophy. Collaboration and interdependence for many are integral parts of what it means to be in sustainable leadership, promoting for some a 'vision of hope, a shared responsibility for future generations, and a call to action on the part of all citizens' (Papa, 2017: 48–9). Nolet (2016) suggests that in stressing sustainability, learners are helped to learn and think collaboratively, and thereby collaboration in itself carries the elements of sustainability that will support a better future. As explained in Chapter 2, system leadership is seen as a means towards a self-improving system in which change for the future is driven by those leading and within the schools, and therefore this is sustainable change. As Middlewood and Abbott (2017) argue, leaders should be role models for sustainability and show their commitment to a sustainable future. Working closely in collaboration with other schools, leaders, staff and learners shows this commitment at first hand. When we referred earlier to leaders having a strong purpose that relates to the best interests of the children and young people concerned, we need to note that this must, of course, include the future generations of those children and young people, which must not be put at risk by any leadership actions taken now.

Openness and transparency

For any effective collaborative practice to succeed, it is imperative that those involved have no secrets from others. Between schools, there needs to be 'a climate of professional generosity and exchange in which leaders open up –' (Craig and Bentley, 2005: 4). While such openness should be at the heart of any effective school culture, it is particularly important for collaborative leaders working across several schools, each of which will have some individual characteristics of its own. With policies to be applied across these schools, the leaders' own approach to their implementation is crucial. Policies are after all based on rational and intellectual processes, but the people who implement them are emotional beings and may have to deal with policies the merits of which they are not totally persuaded. Research (Donaldson-Feilder, Yarker and Lewis, 2011) has found that wearing a 'mask' of feelings at work can cause stress, which can spill over into personal lives. Thus, leaders who recognize the importance of emotional health in staff and themselves are more likely to gain support from staff. As emotions are rarely completely consistent, this implies an acknowledgement that incidents and errors that occur may be inevitable. Of course, leaders themselves are emotional people, and while they wear a 'mask' at times, as anyone else, they need to try to avoid passing on their worst kind of mood to staff. Sy, Cole and Saavedra (2005) found that the transmission of a leader's negative mood had far more impact on staff moods than the other way round. Thus, being open and transparent about school issues is crucial, but the leaders may have to show more self-control than others perhaps.

A key element of the openness needed is in the recognition that other people and schools have as many effective answers to tricky questions as they do. No one owns all these answers. We have previously mentioned the need to recognize the individuality of every single school and that trying to transplant practice that works in one place will not automatically work in another. Effective collaboration works, we have found, when each of those involved, whether across two or six schools, can see the merit in others' attempts. Especially in a market-driven environment within which many schools in developed countries work, collaborative leaders never 'over-sell' their own solutions to raising attainment. Hentschke (2007: 150) describes how low-performing schools in many US urban districts are required to 'buy in' some services from other schools. This can enhance demand, but it can prove to be ineffective if there is pressure to require purchasing services other than those relevant to the original specific needs. The generosity of spirit referred to earlier means that effective professional practices are open to being shared with others and are not some 'secret recipe' for an individual school's success. As such, they are subject to scrutiny, which may enable others to take from them what they feel works in their own context. It is necessary to say, therefore, that openness must include being open about one's failures as well as successes, sharing them and being willing to learn from them so that all those in the collaboration can benefit. Far from being a contradiction of sustainability, this willingness to learn from temporary setbacks is a key indicator of it, as it demonstrates a commitment to remaining steadfast to the longer-term goals and values, being willing to reflect and stay confident in the course they are set on.

Understanding of and commitment to mutual learning

It seems clear that collaboration across schools and across leaders can really only work effectively when it is founded on the recognition that everyone has something to learn from someone else. In the particular case study of a fee-paying and a state school we showed in Chapter 4, the failure was clearly due to the certainty that neither felt they had anything to learn from the other because the two contexts – and perhaps the basic ideologies – were so different. Where there is recognition of the professionalism of leaders, teachers and other staff, there can be that 'absence of dependency' that Arnold (2006) described as vital to successful collaboration across schools. The effective collaborative school leaders stress that they remain learners and have things to learn from other leaders and anyone they work with, and that each school and its staff within any group of schools, regardless of specific structures, has things to learn from others. They believe that in such mutual learning lies the key to ever-improving standards and systems.

Commitment to focused professional development

Understanding that a successful school is always learning and developing is clearly a requirement for all school leaders, but those involved in leading a group of schools were particularly keen on ensuring that such learning has commonalities across all the schools in the group. While there was a recognition of the importance of retaining some of the individuality of each school, collaborative leaders were clear that shared professional development was essential to ensure both high standards and keeping all the schools on the same future path. The training and professional learning, therefore, needed to be focused and based on the carefully identified needs of the people concerned. There is a strong case here for in-house or – in this case – 'in-group' research being carried out by staff – and almost certainly by pupils and students also to ensure that the training needs are identified as being completely relevant. Along with others, Middlewood and Abbott (2015: 23) have argued that context is all-important in developing changes in teaching and learning, and while looking at effective practice elsewhere is clearly sensible, any transplanting of approaches used elsewhere is unlikely to succeed. They point out the importance of 'insider influence' (ibid), and when this can refer to the influence of insiders from five or six schools, it is all the more powerful. Thus, an effective collaborative group is a rich source for practitioner research that can provide precise identification of training needs, and the effective collaborative leader will encourage or even exploit this to the fullest.

Resilience

Again, while all effective school leaders need to be resilient people, able to cope with adversity and setbacks, we see this as essential for effective collaborative leaders. If we accept that resilience is best understood 'as a dynamic within a social system of interrelationships' (Day and Schmidt, 2007: 68), then this dynamic is tested to the full in the complexities of collaborative school structures. Although it is true that some human natures are innately more resilient than others, it is also true that quality can be enhanced by the experiences that are encountered, the kind of contexts within which one operates and the people with whom one works. Thus, we found that effective school leaders believed that their personal resources were actually enhanced by the complexities and difficulties met during the establishing and growing of collaboration with others. Resilience becomes more than merely the ability to 'bounce back' after a setback, important though that is for leadership. It becomes part of what Tugade et al. (2004) described as emerging from the use of positive emotions, such as a love of learning, in a structure of professional relationships as a force for being more creative and constructive. Fresh ideas come from such contexts and school leaders, as they found themselves in situations that they had not met previously, began to have new ideas and proposals for going forward in the collaborative structure. As one leader expressed it,

> You get one idea, then another and whilst all of them will not work, you learn that that is not a failure, so much as a chance to go on to something else. I had often read the dictum about seeing something that has gone wrong as not a failure but an opportunity, and had thought how easy it was to say but it did not stop me feeling a failure! Now, by having worked in these complex set-ups, it has actually meant something real to me.

One of the key features of effective school leaders was their ability to be active, rather than reactive, which we see as an element of resilience. When a situation looked threatening, for example, in relation to a new development in the way the group organization might be structured, they tended to anticipate and see the positive on the horizon. 'As long as you know you are sticking to what is best for the children, you can be confident in what you do about what comes along,' said a leader who was confronted by a potential 'take-over' by a multi-academy trust of the school she led. Her counter-proposals were considered by the trust and played a significant part in the eventual restructuring of the group of schools.

Being effective in prioritizing

This element that came out of interviews with collaborative leaders seems to be strongly related to the difference in scale between leadership of one school and of several schools. Clearly, leaders always have to prioritize from a list of apparently important and sometimes urgent matters that need attention. When the scale of an operation is multiplied by four or five times, it makes sense that that list may be much longer. The task of prioritizing is more critical, and Case example 9A indicates how the problem may not be immediately apparent.

Case example 9A

Sonia was one of three headteachers in a federation of three primary schools in an urban setting in the west of England. She describes how

> In the first few months of the federation coming into being, we met regularly and, although I would say our educational philosophies were all similar, we never seemed to agree about what we should do first. When we did decide, as we had to, there was always at least one of us who was dissatisfied, feeling that what had been decided was not the most needed thing at the time. After a while, I remembered the notion of the difference between something being urgent and something being important. We discussed this and from then on, everything for consideration was put into a category – important, not important, urgent, not urgent, urgent but not important, urgent and important. The first and last categories were the ones that mattered! It changed our way of thinking and enabled us all to justify the agreed federation action back in our individual schools. It helped to make me more reflective and when I later became the overall leader of the group, I found prioritizing much easier. If you do not have this ability, there could potentially be friction regularly between schools.

Note that this particular skill in being effective in prioritizing is closely linked with the characteristic of being reflective, so important for the strategic leader and as noted by Sonia in Case example 9A. As Hamel and Pritchard (1994) noted, there is always business that demands the leader's attention *now*, but we suggest that the effective leader, especially in collaborative situations, will resist the temptation to win admiration for being a man or a woman of action and see the future as of equal importance to the present. If not, 'the capacity to act rather than think or imagine becomes the sole measure for leadership' (ibid: 4–5). The balance between reflection and action is at the core of effective prioritizing. See Case example 9B.

Case example 9B

Colin's experience of being a very successful principal of a school seen as 'outstanding' and being asked to take over the leadership of a failing school exemplifies well in our opinion the strengths of collaborative leadership. In his own words,

> I like to think that times have changed since the days when a new 'super hero' principal would be sent in to the failing school to sort it out or turn it round. Staff would be fired, new resources found, new disciplines imposed including excluding many more pupils, and a new pride in the school established! We now know that such tactics have short term impact but that when the new saviour has departed (usually to collect a knighthood!), after a period, the school regresses.
>
> When I took over this failing school, it was to incorporate it into a group of collaborating schools. Although a tiny number of teachers did leave, there were no new resources but my biggest resource was the other schools in the group! I spent most of my time being in all the schools involved, not just the failing one, meeting and talking with just about everyone about what we were all aiming at together. I organized an extensive programme of exchanges between schools, some for a few days, some for a term, some for a year. Good practice was observed and brought back. Some teachers were absolutely transformed and this was in their attitude as well as their teaching. They were infused with the ethos of the other schools and it made my changes to improve leadership and management processes very straightforward. One small example pleased me most and it was that of a teacher from the failing school who had applied for early retirement and was glad to escape; after spending a term in one of the other schools he withdrew his request and opted to stay on to help the school improve! It did – and the school was graded 'good' at the next inspection.

Achieving a balance of directive and consultative leadership

The above point leads straight into the need for collaborative leaders to be able to strike a balance between knowing when to take firm decisive action through authoritative approaches to a situation and when to take a fully consultative approach. Again, it is well known that effective leaders use a range of leadership styles as appropriate to what the context requires. However, leading across a number of different schools accentuates this need. Several leaders commented on the time issue, so that unless very reliable structures for communication and consultation were in place and could be swiftly activated, full consultation across a group of schools was rarely possible, because policy demands were often requiring responses in a relatively short period of time. The distinction could be made for some between consultation on the longer-term direction of the group and giving clear leadership guidance on matters that were of more immediate importance.

Challenges facing collaborative school leaders

Effective monitoring

Clearly, when operating across two or more schools, leaders will find it increasingly difficult to keep their fingers on the pulse of everything that is happening. The larger the scale, in the sense of the greater the number of schools, the more complex any kind of monitoring system may become. There is also the less formalized, more intuitive aspect of effective leadership, in that successful school principals have 'a nose for', or a sense of what is going on. This is very difficult for leaders involved across and sometimes detached from a number of schools. Inevitably, they have to rely on other sources to alert them to any hidden issues, especially those that have the potential to develop into perhaps a significant problem. The difficulty here is, of course, that no two schools are exactly the same, and what is a problem in one school may not be so in another. Plus, the person who brings it to the leader's attention may have quite a different perspective to that equivalent person in a different school. This whole area is more of a cultural issue than a functional one and raises the question as to what extent can a group of collaborating schools, while having the special ethos of each individual school, develop a recognizable culture of its own? The schools in a group, federation or chain may all operate according to common standards and perhaps to common stated values, but some elements of a school's ethos remain elusive, and can these be agreed and in some sense coordinated?

There is limited evidence in our research, but it is worth noting that in some cases the existence of a genuine 'pupil voice' or 'student voice' reassured leaders that they had access to an authenticity of what are, after all, the most important people in the organization, that is, the learners. We, along with others (Rhodes and Brundrett, 2010; Whitty and Wisby, 2007) see the development of this instrument as one of the most exciting and important issues in education in this century. It is surely not a coincidence that some of the countries that excel in learner attainment, such as the Nordic countries, have well-established mechanisms for the representation of the voice of the learner and, as Mortimore (2013: 206) says, 'is one of the ways in which the next generation of citizens is introduced to democracy'. Here, in collaborative school groups, its potential perhaps remains relatively unexplored. Like most of the other issues however, the voice of the learner can only become more relevant as well as more powerful as schools work ever more closely together.

Balance of support and monitoring

Our research into teaching school alliances in Chapter 6 identified the difficulty for some school leaders in being able to find the right balance between monitoring the progress of fellow leaders and actively intervening to offer and provide support to them. There are similar difficulties for executive leaders in trying to remain in an overall strategic role, and resisting being involved in operational aspects of management of schools in the group, especially when they felt they could clearly perceive an issue that need to be dealt with. This balance – or lack of it – could so easily put a strain on the relationships between leaders and other staff, especially senior staff. Since such relationships are at the heart of effective leadership, the need to achieve the right balance here, between allowing appropriate autonomy and offering necessary support, is crucial. Since autonomy inevitably means the ability to make mistakes, the temptation to intervene to avoid errors is a strong one. In a single school, while encouraging colleagues to take risks and learn from errors is a legitimate leadership approach, the ability to step in directly at any point remains an option that is far more problematic in any collaborative structure.

One of the less-than-clear concepts is the role of the 'leading' school and, therefore, its leader in future collaborative structures. As we have seen in various countries, the notion of using a highly successful school linked with others in order to raise overall levels of achievement is at the heart of various models of collaboration between schools. While the views of school leaders strongly tend to favour mutual learning and partnerships of equals, it is as yet unclear as to whether complete mutuality is possible within such groups in the future, or whether it even necessarily desirable for fully effective collaboration. In the teaching school alliances, we found some evidence of resentment at the perceived superior role of the teaching school and thereby its leaders. How far this will persist is impossible to say at this stage. If the notion of a leading school in the structures of the future persists, then the issue of resource allocation will become significant and require careful and even sensitive handling by the body responsible.

The temptation of 'empire-building'

While none of the school leaders felt they were in any way guilty of expanding their domains to gain more of a field of authority, several of them were both intelligent and sensitive enough to recognize the temptation that could exist for this. As one of them explained in Chapter 8, if the commercial sponsors wanted to add more schools to a group or chain, they would inevitably turn to the serving group leader to take this on. And then a further school? And then another one? Such additional schools are likely to be ones in a vulnerable condition or context, so the motives can either genuinely be or superficially be seen as professionally honourable. Nevertheless, such expansion can have clear dangers, not only for the sponsors and the communities served but also for the collaborative group leader. Case example 9C shows these dangers, as encountered by one individual principal.

Case example 9C

Erica was a principal of a successful secondary school in the north of England, not far from the border with Scotland. When a local secondary school was judged to be failing, she was asked to take on that school in addition to her own. After four years, Erica found herself in charge of a total of five schools, including her original one, and she had become the executive leader of the group of five, each of which had its own leader. During the next year, she was approached by the chair of the governing board of the trust in charge of the five schools, with the 'exciting' news that the trust had agreed to take on three more schools over the next year. Erica describes her feelings:

> I had already become very detached from the daily work of any of the
> schools. There were mountains of paper work and lots of data collection
> and I had to take a good look at myself and what I might become. If I had
> wanted to be an inspector or chief administrator, I could have applied for
> that much earlier. The task was becoming huge and appearing less and
> less to do with educational matters, as it seemed to me. The Board's Chair
> at once said that they knew the job was huge and I could have a Deputy
> Executive, but this of course missed the point completely. I also felt I was
> a little more near cracking point and, although the financial rewards were
> excellent, I had no life to enjoy the benefits of having that kind of money!
> I decided to resign and try to return to being principal of a single school,
> but, to be frank, I think people getting my applications felt that I was
> giving up and, in any case, these single schools were themselves nearly all
> becoming part of various collaborative groups, and people were probably
> suspicious of my motives. So I am taking early retirement!

'Empire-building' as a concept is really about expansion for expansion's sake, and it is probably safe to say that it is a risk more likely to be unseen by sponsors (as in Case example 9C) than by the principals themselves. As Huxham and Vangen (2005) noted, collaboration of any sort ought not to be entered into without a clear purpose that is shared by all parties involved. Power, however, is or can be seductive, and human beings in positions of authority may not be immune sometimes. Furthermore, not only is the temptation of empire-building a reality, but we should note that this is likely to be a perception of some others, even when the leaders themselves are clear that this is not the motive. Being aware that such perceptions will exist is something for collaborative leaders to take account of (see Middlewood and Abbott, 2017: 70–71). One unanswered question at present, particularly pertinent to some current academy chains, is the extent to which school leaders will have more or less autonomy as the chain increases. The possibility that schools in the chain will become more uniform as the numbers grow is a very real one, with consequences for curriculum rigidity, and thereby, of course, for school leadership.

Limited opportunities for collaborative leadership training and development

As noted briefly in Chapter 8, the interviewed school leaders found that the few people trying to provide some kind of training and development for collaborative leaders were only moderately effective and useful to them. The reason for this was, they saw, not because of any inherent inadequacy in the trainers' capabilities, but because the pace of change in the kinds of collaborative structures occurring meant that foreseeing training needs was almost impossible. As earlier chapters have shown, new kinds of ways of schools collaborating regularly occur, and it is very difficult to foresee what form future ones might take. For example, one scenario can envisage groups of schools becoming larger and larger with an executive leadership of several people. Another might foresee a reaction against this growth and, therefore, a return to much smaller units with schools working in pairs or triads perhaps. Also, the issue of whether there could be 'lead' schools in these groups or whether they would all be equal remains unresolved.

This uncertainty, it can be argued, is part and parcel of life in education in the twenty-first century, just as it is in other fields of leadership and management. It means that preparation for leadership roles can only ever be generic in nature, such as in developing relevant skills such as adaptability, change management, risk-taking and so on. It may be worth to highlight one issue relevant to any future training. It is that, without exception, all leaders of groups of schools, large and small, began their leadership experience as principals or headteachers of single schools. There must surely be merit in considering what the significant differences are between leading and managing these schools and leading a school or schools in a collaboration arrangement with other schools. We identified some of these differences earlier, in Chapter 3. Any training and development for collaborative leaders, therefore, should take account of such differences and devise and build programmes accordingly, helping leaders to make the bridge between leading single schools and groups of schools.

A positive aspect in this whole area of training and development was seen as being in the opportunities for leadership experience that offered themselves via the new collaborative structures emerging. These gave chances for leaders and aspiring leaders to gain experience in different schools within the group. Even at principal level, the need to prepare for executive leadership by spending time leading in a different school was essential. Such movements of principals exist already in various countries even without collaborative structures; for example, in some parts of Pakistan, a school principal may be asked to lead a very different kind of school, and appropriate induction and training are provided.

Raising of expectations that may not be realized

This challenge exists in a completely new context where new forms of cross-school structures are emerging. As noted in Chapter 8, several leaders foresaw that as apparently clear routes for professional advancement appeared, so aspiring leaders might see these as the obvious career path. An example is for a deputy principal to become a principal of a single school, then principal of a school in a collaborative group, and then an executive principal. Leaders questioned whether such expectations were realistic in a world where capacity for expansion was limited, and therefore wondered if they might lead to disappointment. Possibly, this is a further issue for future training and development programmes to address.

Conditions essential to success in collaborative school leadership

Finally, we note from our research into the leadership of a range of collaborative school groups what school leaders themselves believed to be essential to enable them to be successful.

- That the collaboration must be based on the notion of a professional partnership, no matter how many were involved.
- These partnerships were based on mutual trust and integrity.
- That there should be an element of negotiation in all partnerships even when the fact of the alliance had been imposed from outside. The form and nature of the partnership should be on terms agreed between those involved.
- That the potential for mutual learning for the collaborating partners should be openly recognized and opportunities for its development should be encouraged.
- That the accountability structures should be made clear from the outset of any collaborative process.
- That there should be clarity as far as possible about the distribution or allocation of resources within and across the collaboration.

Summary

This chapter has:

- made comments on models of collaborative leadership;
- briefly noted some factors that are common to all effective school leadership;
- presented some features that are significant in the effectiveness of collaborative school leadership;
- identified some of the challenges facing collaborative school leaders; and
- noted the conditions believed by the school leaders themselves to be necessary for effective collaborative school leadership to take place.

Recommended reading

Arnold, R. (2006). *Schools in collaborations*. EMIE Report no 86. Slough: National Foundation for Educational Research. This research-based report on the state of play in collaboration between schools in the relatively early days sets out some key principles, and some 'do's' and 'dont's' that are relevant.

Miller, P., and Hutton, D. (2014). Leading from within to a comparative view. In S. Harris, and J. Mixon (eds), *Building cultural communities*. Ypsilenti: NCPEA. This chapter examines the elements in leadership in an organization and shows how they may be related to effective working in a leading role in the external environment.

Chapter 10
Collaborating Communities: A Realistic Vision?

Introduction

In this book, we have considered the leadership of schools in various forms of collaborative working with other schools. While each individual school is in itself a community, the group of schools hopefully form some kind of learning community, whether in a fairly concentrated urban area, or a 'chain' of schools that are geographically apart but linked through other means. However, all schools are themselves part of other kinds of societal, regional, local or neighbourhood communities that the school serves. When schools collaborate, this clearly has implications for such communities and also raises questions about how they can be effectively led. This chapter therefore:

- considers the implications for social communities affected by collaborating schools;
- discusses the potential for collaboration across such communities;
- considers the implications for schools and some of their stakeholders;
- debates what kind of leadership is required for their development and how school leadership can best contribute to this; and
- finally suggests a possible route for the future of school leadership in this context.

Social communities

Education is not necessarily an end in itself, except perhaps for individual bet-terment. In wider terms, it is surely something to do with the improvement or development of people, the world, the country, society and the local community. Major changes for the better are mostly achieved effectively neither at national level, where they may be seen as 'counter-productive' (Hargreaves, 2010: 34), nor at individual level or small scale where they are likely to be 'inadequate' (ibid). Rather, the locus of power for change is at community level (Brock, 2011: 35). Changes at community level tend to be more enabling, as opposed to national ones that are normally prescriptive. Communities are where we live, work and learn; and in the future perhaps, we should be thinking about developing the community and what part schools can play in this, rather than focusing exclu-sively on schools as institutions trying to achieve success in the 'technical' aspects of learning and teaching, as assessed through tests and examinations. Such an idea is justified in that we already know through research in a range of fields that schools – and indeed all educational institutions and formal educa-tion systems – are just one of the various contributors to success in learning – an important factor certainly, but only one factor. We know very well that mental and physical health, reasonable prosperity, satisfying employment, safe environ-ment, adequate housing and fulfilling relationships, all have a huge impact on the effectiveness of humans' learning and development, just as the absence of all or some of them can have a devastatingly and even dysfunctional negative influence. Schools are, therefore, ideally seen as part of a community's educa-tion and learning provision and will continue to be so. The focus at some point in the future, however, may need to be on the community's development and the extent to which schools can contribute to that, and this may be the issue for the future in terms of how we think about a school and what it does for its clients. This obviously has huge implications for school leadership, and we shall return to this later in the chapter.

In considering what we mean by a community, we need to resist any simplistic definitions. In the past, with the school as central, it might mean a neighbour-hood area around a school, but at least two factors show this to be an irrelevant description:

- Firstly, consider how a school comes about. A new area is developed and only then is a school needed – the community is first, then the school. It is needed to serve the community, just as the area needs shops, eating places and other service providers.

- Second, in more developed countries, the development of a market-oriented model of school choice has meant that, as parents exercise choice by their children attending schools at a distance, the dislocation of many schools from their local or immediate neighbourhood is significant, so that an individual school does not serve one particular community because its learners live in several different communities.

In any case, simplistic descriptions of particular communities can be misleading. Factors such as history, culture, population composition, all affect the way a community develops. If one makes simple assumptions about values being shared across a community, this may take no account of not only differences or inequalities between each stakeholder group but also of differences or inequalities *within* each group. Middlewood and Parker (2009: 29) give an interesting account of a social worker's interviews with residents of a particular urban community in England about how they came to be living there. The interviewees ranged from seventeen to ninety-one in age, and the answers included:

'I was born and bred here, and my parents before me.'

'We came here as a young couple but hate it now but can't escape.'

'What makes you think we chose to come here? We were put here.'

'Who would actually choose to live in a dump like this?'

Thus, communities can be complex webs of relationships and systems of power and beliefs, and it is necessary to understand something of the dynamics that influence people's choices and decisions. In various countries in Africa and Asia, these dynamics can involve deeply rooted questions of identity connected to historic ties. A political correspondent, who had witnessed electoral polls in Nepal and Bangladesh, referred to the role of 'clan, caste, tribe, ethnicity, importance of identity' in affecting how people voted (Burke, 2016: 18). Western observers often struggle to understand local factional rivalries in such countries, but Burke suggested that the vote to leave the European Community in the 2016 referendum in the UK had similarly much to do with such local identities and 'tribal' allegiances that overcame the received wisdom of national governments and political parties.

Also, where environments are unstable, collaboration is clearly more difficult, and while instability can relate to socioeconomic or political issues in many developed countries, more extreme forms of instability can make it almost impossible. Abaya (2016: 761) not only describes the impact of 'ethnic violence between two warring tribes' on the quality of school leadership in an area of Kenya, but refers to various factors causing instability in Ghana, Zambia, Sudan and Rwanda. In such situations, collaboration between communities is highly unlikely, although it does not rule out collaboration between schools and their leaders as an opportunity for increased positive relationships.

If it is true, or even partially so, that real change may occur at the level of localism, the potential for members of a community to come together for a cause that unites them – or for something they feel they have common cause in – is something perhaps that educationalists need to try to access and is a challenge for leaders to achieve. Thus, a community may be seen as arising from a general sharing of beliefs and values that people come to have and the realization of this through social relations and interactions.

Collaboration within and across communities

Collaboration is crucial to establishing and sustaining success in and for communities, because, without it, success for one part of the community will likely be at the expense of the failure or underperformance of some other parts. Collaboration has been at the heart of effective schools and, as shown in earlier chapters of this book, of effective performance of groups of schools. As noted earlier, the quasi-market nature of educational systems in some countries has led to some schools being perceived as highly successful, and this has meant others have become failing or underperforming ones. In some cases, the movement of more able children to schools in more affluent areas has meant that the areas with the failing schools become perceived as poorer areas, and thus the division is both increased and perpetuated. Perhaps, for those striving towards a truly collaborative and effective community, the following should be aimed for:

- support being available throughout the whole of the community to enable everyone to develop;
- identification of needs to be done by those within the community;
- gradual elimination of a sense of dependency on outside agencies to resolve issues; and
- the community itself to become an agency for change.

Putnam (2000: 297) believed that places – of any social stratum – whose residents trust each other, join local organizations, volunteer, vote and socialize are ones where children flourish, and claimed that 'the correlation between high social capital and positive child development is as close to perfect as social scientists ever find in data analysis of this sort'.

We believe there are important lessons to be drawn from the community schools movement in Scotland and similarly in the United States, and also from the extended schools movement in England and Wales. All these initiatives focussed on engaging the local community through various forms of integrated provision of services and the involvement of community members in the provision and management of services. Residents in a community began to see schools not just as places where children went to be taught but as places where other considerations of daily life could be addressed. Dryfoos et al. (2005) felt that the key one of all these was health, both physical and mental – 'health, dental and mental health ser-vices, home-based early head-start, and day care, after school and teen programs, summer camp programs, weekend and holiday programs, family life and sex education, parent education' (p. 14). The natural place for this provision to be centred on was the local neighbourhood school. Similarly, in England and Wales, some extended schools (especially those known as full-service extended schools) provided a similar range of such services, and some, which tended to be in slightly more prosperous areas, included gymnasia, hairdressing salons and beauty salons, as well as career advice provision for adults. A change of government in UK meant the disappear-ance of funding support for extended schools and thereby some of that integrated provision.

However, those systems also have potential drawbacks. No matter how dedi-cated the school staff may be, there may be members of parts of the community who will not see the particular school as 'their' place to go. Middlewood and Parker (2009) found in their research into effective extended schools that offer-ing some services away from school, even in apparently unlikely places, greatly increased the chances of community response. Furthermore, Hall Jones (2003) points out that the provision of every possible avenue for individuals' develop-ment can sometimes backfire, by making them feel that their own inability and depression is magnified by the plethora of every opportunity, leading to feelings of inadequacy and being unworthy of self-respect.

In discussing ways forward for community development, Dyson (2006: 99) suggested that some strategies may involve focussing on what peo-ple cannot do – their low aspirations, disengagement from learning, poor parenting skills – and trying 'to find ways of changing these negative or dys-functional aspects of individuals and families'. Others may focus on 'the disadvantaging conditions and limited opportunities that people experience and set about changing these external circumstances rather than the people themselves' (ibid). Todd (2007) argues strongly that any kind of deficit model is ultimately doomed to fail as it can only be short-term; that is, by focus-ing on the problems, people are not encouraged to see beyond the fixing of the problem to a positive view of what might be. It is important that people are not just seen in terms of their problems – 'The problem is the problem' (p. 137). She gives as an example of community control over decision mak-ing the use of family group conferences (FGCs). This process is based on the Maori community process and is used in New Zealand, the UK and in sev-eral other countries. In this process, family strengths rather than deficits are valued, family members are centred as knowledgeable, creative solutions are generated, and collaboration is fostered 'within families and between families and professionals' (ibid: 153). Timperley and Robinson (1998) do not see any of this as diluting professionalism in any way and suggest it is a kind of 'com-munitarian democracy' (p. 167).

Implications for schools and their stakeholders

What part might schools play in such collaborative communities, both in help-ing to bring them about and then as elements within them? There is surely only limited capacity for more improvement in school systems, although we always want schools, like any other organizations, to strive to be better. School improve-ment is necessary but is a long way from being *the* key to improving and indeed educating a society or community. Clearly, schools need to model collaboration, both internally through the way it operates, and externally though its relation-ship with its environment. The widely different cultures within which education systems operate in various countries make it very difficult to generalize, but per-haps the following can be suggested:

- Schools need to perceive themselves as less of an institution and as more of an agency (West-Burnham, 2000).

- They recognize themselves as one of the contributors to life-long learning, which in selected cases has a focus on the earlier years ('early years' here being the first eighteen years of life, which is likely to be about a hundred years in the future in the developed world!).

- They understand that the most effective learning is that which comes about through 'engagement with the community in carefully articulated partner-ships' (Dryfoos et al., 2005: 221), and trying to do everything on one's own has proved to be a doomed approach.

- They understand that the success of *all* schools is as crucial as the success of any individual school, and therefore, working with and for others is a necessity.

- They see themselves as places where community members play a full part in the operation of the school in a variety of roles, paid and voluntary – any role except that of the teacher (who has been specifically trained in the specialism of teaching). As mentioned earlier, the increase in para-professionals can mean that the experience and skills of community mem-bers in the pastoral and emotional welfare of younger learners can be fully used. (See Middlewood et al., 2005: 58, for examples of the use of non-teaching staff in a school, where their experience as brothers, aunts and grandfathers enables them, with training, to become effective tutors for young people aged fourteen to eighteen.)

- They realize that part of their role is to broker change in the community but also to cede some issues or resources for the greater good of that community.

- We shall consider leadership in the later sections of this chapter, but all the above relates to all those people involved with the school as stakeholders in one form or another. Implications for teachers would require a whole book(!) and is not our topic here, of course. There is space here briefly to consider the implications for only two of a school's key stakeholders – governors and parents. School governance varies widely from country to country, but – and there is evidence of this already in examples in earlier chapters of this book – there is likely to be an increase in governors serving groups of schools rather than individual ones. Representation of local interests would be less parochial, and the agenda brought by governors could be more about what this school can bring to the community rather than what we can bring to the school as members of the community. This practice of identification of community needs being considered in the light of how a school could meet them is certainly present in the best practice of community and extended schools, but would go further in that any school could be considered, and the one best placed to deliver would be chosen.

Our case examples in this chapter involve different people with relevant experience being interviewed about issues being debated here. Case example 10A concerns Ken who has been a school governor in England for more than sixteen years. He has served on governing bodies of nursery, primary and secondary schools and acted as a parent governor, a community governor and later as a local council representative. How does he think governors' roles would change?

Case example 10A

Every school I know is in some form of collaborative network or partnership – one school I work with is in eight different kinds of partnership! Three of 'my' schools have joint governing bodies. It is very difficult to keep track of what is going on and who is driving what. I find the only way to make sense of it all in this complexity is to ensure you keep the focus on one thing above anything else when you attend a governors' meeting – and that is –how is the learning of those in this school progressing? The children mainly, but also the staff and of course us! After all, the children's education is statutory and the rest are not, so you could say by law we must do that. If the nature of schools changes, children's education will still be statutory because they are the future adults, parents, and community members. Even if you put the community first and schools are just a part, I would still argue that children remain the key, especially the early years ones. We know that children spent more time at home than they do at school, so school is only a part of their lives, although very important. I favour much more parent and children learning together models or family learning and hope this will become more central over the years. I also worry about the generational gap as populations age and think school governors need to be of all ages in the future, from

> eighteen to eighty. My thought about the biggest thing to be overcome is
> the narrowness of outlook of some governors through the fierce allegiance
> they can have to a local school, and this is also why I favour not having
> parent governors – they tend to think first of their own children!

Ken's final comment is relevant in that the UK government is proposing to abolish parent representation on school governing bodies in England, although there is no evidence that it is for the reasons Ken suggests. His other comment about generational gaps as populations age is something that has been identified by the US Search Institute back in 2000 as part of the reasons for a 'crumbling infrastructure', based to a large extent on mistrust and suspicion brought about by a lack of contact and communication.

The implications for parents may include that:

- they may well be involved in several schools, not just the one(s) attended by their children, and groups of parents from different schools may come together much more often as 'common cause' community groups;

- more importantly, many will be recognized and respected for their other roles in the community that are not obviously connected with school. They may be respected as community contributors, whether as professionals, volunteers or para-professionals. There will be a huge increase in the last group in the community with the majority of people being able to have training to a level of competence in various fields that support the community.

For any or all of the above to develop, leadership is needed, and we now turn our attention to this.

Leadership of schools and the community

Twenty-first-century thinking about educational leadership accepts that there must be a moral purpose that underpins it all (Davies, 2007; Fullan, 2003, 2005). This moral purpose we may define here as the social regeneration of a community or communities, based on social justice and equity. The new collaborative leadership will perhaps ultimately lie in a kind of collective leadership capacity within the community. The family group conferences, mentioned earlier, are possibly an example of this, as there are no specified individual leaders involved in this kind of process. It is interesting to speculate whether this constitutes a kind of extended distributed leadership, often described as the most popular leadership model of the twenty-first century (e.g. Bush, 2016: 712). The debate about the merits of distributed leadership can centre on whether it is allowed to emerge through a particular kind of organizational culture, or whether the leadership tasks have to be allocated, such as described in the example of Singapore (Yuen et al., 2016), within a highly centralized educational system.

Challenges facing the new leaders include:

- Being able to release control and focus on enabling and facilitating others, as leadership capacity is enhanced. This is difficult for some, perhaps for quite a number of people. As Dreyfoos et al. (2005: 261) stress, 'Not everyone is a born collaborator. Some have to acquire the skills and others just do not know or want to know how to work intensively with others.' West-Burnham (2005: 105) describes this shift in thinking and practice as a movement away from 'personal status towards recognition of leadership as a collective capacity'.

- Being able to move thinking away from the insularity of outlook of both individual schools and even of groups of schools. The quasi-market education system in several developed countries has established a climate of competition between schools, which even in more collaborative times may be hard for some school leaders to ignore. A focus on school performance improvement that is inevitably concerned with internal structures and processes within the institution can be difficult to change for a focus on the external. In some African and Asian regions, where the local community has been a more obvious agency for bonding the various elements in education of children, this local loyalty can militate against attempts to collaborate with other communities. In one South African province, and also in a Tanzanian one, Middlewood et al. (2016) found that school principals felt hugely isolated, which was alleviated when their contact with other principals in other areas was facilitated. Occasionally, such contacts met initial opposition from such community members as tribal elders, who held influence locally.

- One of the hardest shifts in thinking for school leaders to adapt to, after decades of being enjoined to ensure the development of their vision for the school, may be in being asked in effect, 'How does the vision for the school fit into the community's vision?' As noted earlier, the community comes first, then the school! Thus, Barber (2005) has questions: 'Who are your key stakeholders in the local community? Do they understand your vision? Are they committed to it?' We believe these should become: 'Do you (the school leaders) understand the community's vision? Are you committed to it?' This, of course, presupposes that school leaders themselves as important community members have played their own part, along with everyone else in helping to form and articulate the community's vision! Case example 10B gives the views of Sheila, an executive principal of a group of five schools in an urban environment.

Case example 10B

We (i.e. our group of schools) believe we have done a good job so far in improving standards within all of the schools and also making a powerful contribution to all the communities served by the schools. We see our job as ultimately improving the whole area affected by our schools so that our school leavers will want to stay and live and work here. Originally, most young people couldn't wait to leave but we have had a lot of ideas about getting adults involved and young ones too. For example, we gave jobs as learning mentors to a dozen young graduates from the area who had not secured jobs on graduating and they came in and were paid to support our current sixteen year olds. Both sides loved it – these people were so much closer in age than most of us and could empathize really well. Some of them went into teaching and others got other jobs – in the area! We want them all not to see this area as one to escape from but one to live in and help the next generation. It is obviously a long term aim but I feel we have made progress. Another development is that adult learning groups are now meeting in all sorts of places – a school will be just one of them. I and my husband wanted to learn some basic Turkish for a holiday we planned and we found ourselves doing a class in a local football team's training centre. Nobody knew who I was – it was great! Initiatives are coming from all over the place – some ideas are a bit off the wall but many lead to something real. I see many of the former students of local primary and secondary schools taking responsibility in community matters in the future. Eventually, I hope that when there is a sudden drop in standards in a school one year, the community will not automatically blame the school, but people will look at themselves and ask what they could have done better. Perhaps that's a pipe dream and we are nowhere near that yet, but already I do feel much less pressure than when I was first principal of a single school. So fingers crossed!

Factors that are positive signs

Although the challenges are considerable, the earlier chapters have shown a number of promising indications of school leadership embracing collaboration across schools, and there are several factors extant that also suggest progress on the way to enabling schools to play their part in communities collaborating. These are some of the features that are commonly found in effective schools today (not in any particular order of priority or importance):

- A concern with sustainability. Writers such as Fullan (2005), Davies (2007) and Papa and Saiti (2016) stress the importance of change being sustainable and an essence of sustainability is not causing harm to others, and being aware of the consequences for others including future generations in actions taken. This concern, therefore, fits perfectly with the notion of people collaborating within and across communities. Effective schools already are developing internal cultures that place emphasis on sustainability, and Middlewood and Abbott (2016), in their study of such cultures, found that the schools' links with their communities were some of the most significant indicators of a commitment to sustainability.

- Devolving leadership responsibility. The sharing of leadership responsibilities in schools, sometimes referred to as distributed leadership, has been of interest to both practitioners and academics. Although academics, in particular, argue about the reality of such distribution, essentially the recognition that leadership can be about expertise rather than the holding of posts of formal authority is both relevant and encouraging for community leadership. It is also worth noting that countries such as the Netherlands and the Nordic countries have been fearful of increasing the power of individual school leaders, according to Mortimore (2013), in the belief that the key role in educational leadership is one of coordination rather than overseeing. The idea that leadership will have many different spheres and centres of influence fits with the idea of communities being led by different people or groups within the community that is seriously engaged with its core purposes.

- Student voice. The prevalence of student or pupil voice in the most effective schools gives not only encouragement to the learners' engagement with the curriculum and education in general, but enhances again the potential for such voices being heard in the community and increasingly for them to take leading roles. Already in the Nordic countries, student voice is the norm in educational organizations, is mandatory in some of these countries, and is possibly part of the reasons why such countries are consistently rated among the highest performing nations. Mortimore (2013: 206) notes that it is 'one of the ways in which the next generation of citizens is introduced to democracy'.

- Personalized learning. The twenty-first-century focus on personalized – as opposed to institutionalized – learning is another crucial step on the path towards community-based learning. In this, the integrity of the individual learner's experience is what matters, and the specific context far less important. The experience within schools at present is perhaps laying the foundations for this, as those schools strive to enable their learners to learn at their own pace and in their own style.

- Diversity and inclusion. This is a massive element for additional focus in educational thinking and practice since the 1990s, and nothing could better illustrate the need for communities to cohere around a diverse number of spheres rather than simply a school. This focus on valuing the widest possible range of people and experiences is central to the way that many effective schools try to develop their organizational cultures, in a significant number of countries.

This list could be added to of course, but there are sufficient indicators here to suggest that the movement towards collaborative communities may be built on a solid foundation and that schools and their leaders may be able to overcome those difficulties mentioned above. Furthermore, there is another aspect of the potential new kind of leadership that can be seen as positive. A huge concern in many countries in the early twenty-first century is the lack of potential future school leaders with decreases in numbers of those applying for principal posts. This has led to great interest in leadership succession planning and in building leadership capacity to ensure there are sufficient educational leaders in the future. The leadership in the community, far from adding to the problem, has the potential to alleviate it because:

- With leadership diffused throughout the communities, the need for highly specialized institutional leaders is decreased, while the quality of leadership is maintained.
- Career development for school leaders is likely to become less restricted and more open, as lateral or sideways movements between posts would become the norm, with much decreased pressure on people to pursue a relentlessly upward or hierarchical route, as advocated by Bentley and Craig (2006). There is evidence of this change in the various leadership posts and roles identified and .discussed in Chapter 8 of this book.

Where will leadership operate and who will be the leaders?

The ideal answer is that leadership will be found anywhere it is needed in the communities, and, equally ideally, leadership becomes more of a 'collective capacity' (West-Burnham, 2006: 105). This does not mean leadership has suddenly become easy! Specialist leadership of classrooms and of schools will still be absolutely vital and require specialist training. The crucial challenge to schools will be in being able to answer the questions:

- What are you doing about this issue that has arisen in our community?
- Is your preparation of these children and young people appropriate for what we have agreed in our community?
- Are you playing your full part in helping us to achieve our community vision? What more could you do?

These indicate such a radical shift from traditional thinking about leadership of schools that it clearly cannot happen quickly. It may be viewed as overidealistic, but then the huge emphasis on leadership for sustainability is necessarily and surely rightly based on an optimistic view of the future. The alternatives are unthinkable!

Case example 10C supports some of that optimism and also warns of the potential dangers of not making the right changes.

Case example 10C

Pam was principal of a high school in New Zealand before retiring in 2016 and had this to say:

> As I left my school after seven years of principalship, there were many things I could reflect on with pride. The way the school was completely open to all members of the local community, the incredible diversity and inclusion of everyone, staff, parents, children, governors and neighbours, the positive culture with a commitment to achievement for everyone and the collaboration with other schools, both locally, nationally and even internationally. In a country that feels vulnerable in the modern climate change context, we had successfully fostered a 'do no harm' ethos in our school and in working with others. AND YET? I shall only know how embedded such things are as I live my retirement and progress into old age as, with luck, my faculties as an intelligent citizen intact. I worry that so many adults still seem immune to making their own decisions! Are they so relaxed, and happy that somebody else will do it for them? Has my leadership, so lauded by others apparently, actually not made them to be able and willing to take a lead themselves? When I am much older and increasingly dependent on others, will I find that the leadership I have dreamed of will be there in society at large or will we be open to the typical 'strong man (or woman)' of history simply taking over. More questions than answers, I know, but perhaps there always will be! I suppose it is when we stop asking the questions that we really have to worry!

What do you think? We can surely agree with Pam's final statement, and therefore, if the chapters have raised the questions, perhaps it is the readers who can give their own answers.

One reservation that is expressed about any system of managed collaborative groups is that it may be seen as 'controlled by an elite even more remote from the influence of representative democracy' (Hatcher, 2008: 30). It is possible that the emphasis placed on communities, as discussed in this chapter, may be seen as more democratic and more dynamic.

School leadership in collaborating communities

Of course, leaders of schools will continue to be needed, and it seems clear that their ability to be collaborative leaders will be a prerequisite in a context where the actual communities of which the schools are part are themselves working together. Some of the issues that will need to be addressed include the following:

Accountability

The need to enable a robust form of accountability remains crucial, and school leaders have their role in contributing to this kind of democratic accountability. As Bush (2016: 711) noted, while it is to be applauded that schools are being set free and operating away from national or regional control, 'the reality is that accountability pressures often increase to match the enhanced autonomy'. Any form of such democratic accountability would ideally:

- be open and transparent;
- be trusted by all those affected;
- offer local groups the opportunity to develop their own forms of account-ability specific to the context that they know best;
- include a large amount of self-evaluation; and
- be flexible enough to be regularly adapted to any context in fast-changing circumstances. (Adapted from Middlewood and Parker, 2009: 73)

If one agrees that the aim of education, through its institutions, communities, leaders, teachers and learners, is to produce a confident society, then we can agree with Bottery (2004: 193) that, looking beyond the current stress on per-formance measurement in quantitative terms, such 'a society would be capable of knowing when to trust and when to demand an audited account'.

School culture

The need for developing an ethos of trust and one where there is a 'no blame and shared credit' culture remains central to effective school leadership, and the accountability models suggested above contribute to this. The task of the school leaders is to ensure all this and the involvement of and collaboration with a large range of stakeholders while ensuring the focus is maintained on the core aim of effective learning. The risk of 'over-collaboration' can be in 'over-consultation', leading to inertia rather than action! However positive the relationships are within the schools' and communities' networks, there will still be the leader's role 'where the need to direct at times and prompt people to move out of personal comfort zones remains crucial' (Middlewood, 2010: 146).

Recruitment and selection

This important area of leadership expertise needs to be significantly more collaborative than it has often been in the past, without being bureaucratically unwieldy. More stakeholders will need to be involved, as the flexibility of those employed in schools continues to increase, in terms of who they are, the hours they operate in, the work they do, the contracts they enjoy and indeed every aspect of staffing. As school collaboration increases, there is clearly a greater likelihood that staff may be appointed to a chain or network of schools rather than an individual one. This has considerable benefits for personnel both in circumstances where an excellent teacher could help in a less successful school or a borderline performer might be more effective in a different institutional context. Such considerations need to be reflected on in any recruitment and selection process.

Summary

This chapter has:

- considered the implications for social communities affected by collaborating schools;
- examined the potential for collaboration within and across communities;
- discussed the possible implications for some of the relevant stakeholders;
- debated the kind of leadership desirable in these communities; and
- briefly considered the implications for school leadership in this context.

Recommended reading

Brock, C. (2011). Epilogue [final chapter in the book]. *Education as a global concern.* London: Continuum. This chapter gives an overview of various universal issues and developments and places special emphasis on the importance of partnerships as a key element in addressing global problems.

West-Burnham, J. (2000). Educational leadership and the community. In T. Gelsthorpe and J. West-Burnham (eds), *Educational leadership and the community.* London: Pearson Education.

Chapter 11
The Future: Possibilities and Practicalities

Introduction

After examining the new collaborative structures in groupings of schools and carrying out research into the leadership of several of these, we now try to look at the picture that has emerged. This chapter therefore:

- reflects on the broader issues underpinning collaborative approaches in education;
- summarizes the findings overall from the earlier research and tries to draw some conclusions from these findings;
- suggests some implications for future developments; and
- offers some ideas for action at various levels that may be useful.

Collaboration in education

'Collaboration across schools is a necessity rather than an optional extra' (Desforges, 2006: 2). These words possibly set out the way ahead for schools in the twenty-first century, and, as Miller (2017: 12) suggests, this will be not only in developed countries but as true for 'developing countries, albeit in different ways'.

In the turbulent global context of the second decade of the twenty-first century and onwards, collaboration per se is seen by many as inevitable. This is partly because it is seen as ultimately more efficient and effective in the new knowledge economy: 'It is more productive to collaborate and share knowledge with one another than to approach it by ourselves' (Gee, 2002: 77). Many others see it also as a moral imperative. This is because it fosters interdependence and thus gives the best opportunity to encourage harmony as compared with hostility; it should, therefore, underpin and 'drive educational policy and principles' (Santone, 2017: 61). In a period where international comparisons are widely made and scrutinized by national governments, such writers make the point that the PISA tables, for example, can be valuable for enabling countries to learn from each other in order to improve education for all, rather than looking to see how one country can outdo another. Such advocates of collaboration are not against competition in itself, only the kind of competition that necessarily requires some to be disadvantaged. In many countries, the market basis for education has seen this disadvantaged sector increase at what some would see as an alarming rate.

Within schools themselves, while teaching is an overall individual practice when it takes place in the classroom, teachers are known to enjoy participating in collaboration with others – through debate, discussion, mutual learning and development, joint practitioner research, and many other activities. Thus, collaboration is perhaps a natural part of learning and teaching organizations, more so than in a number of other professions. However, the collaborative structures that have emerged in various countries and which were described in Chapter 1 are, of course, of a different nature. Some might argue that collaboration works with schools when it is voluntary, and that 'forced' collaboration is alien to teachers, leading to 'contrived collegiality' (Fullan and Hargreaves, 1992: 71). The nature of these new structures that require schools to collaborate leads those such as Hatcher (2008: 30) to question whether they provide a new landscape that is either

> more participatory, more democratic, more dynamic

or

> hierarchical and controlled by a technocratic managerial elite even more remote from the influence of representative democracy?

Whichever or whatever the truth of these turns out to be, we can be certain that the effectiveness of such structures for the benefit of children, education and society will depend on what research has shown to be the two most significant factors in all improvement, that is, the quality of the learning and teaching in the schools and the quality of the leadership and management in and of them. Trying to identify the factors in the second of these, as this book has attempted, is of crucial importance.

What do the findings show?

It would be foolish to deny that a number of schools in our research had been positively transformed, since leaving an authority's network and becoming part of a federation, chain or trust. Many apparently failing schools were now thriving, as were their leaders, staff, parents and pupils. Even in some situations where the move to become an academy had been 'forced', there were success stories, in no small part due to the leaders who, having been reluctant, showed their true professionalism by focussing on the children's needs and achieving what was best for them, despite the reservations they had about the move to becoming an academy, for example. This research and this book is not about the politics of these changes and whether the reasons for the changes were appropriate, but about how the leadership of schools in these new contexts can best work.

We should stress at the outset that most of the groupings of schools described and researched in the book are still at developmental stages. Indeed, several of these groupings were evolving as the book was being written. As several of the school leaders who we interviewed were clear about, these were 'early days' and some saw them as experimental. The confusion about the titles adopted by different groups for their leaders, as shown especially in Chapters 5 and 8, simply highlights the fact that no particular structure has been established as the 'finished article'. It also means we are dealing with a relatively new breed of school leaders, and there is insufficient experience as yet to be certain either of the exact nature of future collaborative structures or the roles that their leaders take.

It does seem clear that many of the skills required by school leaders to be effective in leading collaborative schools will be similar to those required for leading single schools. This is hardly surprising since some leadership qualities can be seen as universal. These include ones such as leading and managing people, using emotional intelligence, monitoring and evaluating, maintaining high-quality teaching and learning, developing strong professional relationships, inspiring others, and implementing changes seen as necessary for everyone's benefit. As we noted in an earlier chapter, this new context for school leadership is not simply about doing the same thing, but doing it on a bigger scale. For example, as some of our interviewed leaders already had found, developing a clear vision for a collective of several diverse schools and communicating that vision effectively and empowering colleagues to enable its fulfilment is a completely different process from doing this in a single school. Each individual school has its own identity, and therefore, the commitment to a clearly stated and understood set of values that underpin the processes across the whole group becomes crucial. These values are, in education, based on key moral purposes that underpin provision for children and young people and are sustainable for future generations as well as those in the schools at present.

School leaders working in these collaborative settings need to have a different mindset from that which was suited to leading an individual school. This is a mindset that begins with a commitment to the wider educational system and its place within the wider society of which it forms part. At the very least, this relates to society at a national level, and increasing probably to the wider world. Schools in these contexts are viewed less as institutions and more perhaps as agencies (West-Burnham, 2006) whose focus is education. Thus, it is hardly surprising that when we summarized some desirable qualities for effective collaborative leadership earlier, in Chapter 9, the ability to see the big picture and think strategically was fundamental.

Future developments

As mentioned earlier, it is uncertain what the structural form of cross-school collaborations may take. However, as with all educational institutions and organizations, what will be of crucial importance is the culture that develops within and across them. Hargreaves and Fullan (2012: 119) stress that 'building collaborative cultures is a patient developmental journey' and 'there are no easy short cuts' (ibid), and Stevenson (2007: 31) sees collaboration as 'time-hungry'. We can consider some of the issues that seem likely to emerge and some of the questions that all those concerned will need to ask and perhaps answer.

What will happen to schools that are not collaborating?

If collaboration becomes the norm, what will happen to so-called 'orphan' schools, the ones that nobody wants to collaborate with? If some schools, which may be viable in terms of numbers, are such that no sponsor or other body wishes to incorporate them into a collaborative group, what will be their fate? Equally pertinent here is the question as to who will lead them? There is evidence in England, at least at present, that such schools may be left in limbo until some kind of 'saviour' appears! The lack of clarity about governance and responsibility in this area is a concern because of the situation of the pupils and the staff while this state exists.

Will there be competition in the collaboration?

It seems slightly illogical to imagine that, if all schools in a country were in some kind of collaborative group, there would not be some form of competition between those actual groups. Some would argue that human nature makes this inevitable, and, in any case, comparisons would be certain to be made. The issue, therefore, is whether it matters, to which the answer surely is – as we noted earlier on international comparison tables – only if it means that some groupings are seen as losers. If, on the other hand, groups can learn from each other, just as individual schools have, then only positives can come from this. As for competition within the collaborative structures, it is likely that some leaders may encourage this and others frown upon it, according to personal beliefs. The biggest risk to progress may be in any groups where a recognized or designated 'leading' feels challenged by others in the group, which could be to the detriment of the whole collaborative structure.

What impact will there be on school leaders' career paths?

We mentioned earlier that at senior level there might appear to be a logical progression from leader of single school, to leader of a group of schools, to executive leader. We also noted that so-called 'sideways' moves in posts might be seen as perfectly feasible and positive, rather than somewhat negatively as they have been in the past. This is because teachers moving across to other schools in the same collaborative group could be seen as both reasonably easy to facilitate and also to gain a range of experience. There are already arrangements in charter schools and some academies whereby staff are appointed to the chain or group, rather than a single school, and this trend is likely to grow. Clearly, this also brings with it the likelihood of contracts for fixed periods in particular posts, something common in some countries and states, and rare in others. There seems to be no evidence from some of the countries that do practice this approach, whether for principals (in some Australian and Canadian states) or for new teachers (as in Tokyo, for example), that it is destabilizing for the profession as a whole.

Will leaders of collaborative groups necessarily need to be teachers?

The argument here is that those in overall charge of a group of schools needing to have a detached and strategic view of the whole enterprise are equivalent to managing directors in the world of business, who are sometimes appointed to oversee a field in which they have no specialist background. As schools, and especially groups of schools with commercial sponsors, are essentially corporations, perhaps no knowledge of the everyday business is needed. However, while it is true that in manufacturing there are successful precedents for an 'outsider' becoming the overall leader, we argue that parallels should be sought more in fields akin to education where the basic 'product' is the welfare and development of the 'client'. Middlewood (2013), after considering key differences between educational and business leadership in terms of outcomes, accountability and workforce composition, suggests that school leadership necessarily is about both process and product. In the UK, the approach of trying to make the National

Health Service more effective and efficient by employing large numbers of managers from outside the health sector was found to be ineffective. This was because of the lack of knowledge and insight of many of those managers, who, while they had skills in bureaucratic procedures and perhaps strategic resource management, had little understanding of what needs that were to be met at an individual level. In both health and education, the recognition of the needs of the individual client, whether patient or pupil, is paramount.

What are the funding implications?

As has been argued from earlier research, certainly some savings need to be made by purse holders through the economies of scale possible through collaborative practices. Apart from the obvious gains from the purchasing of resources on a much bigger scale and bringing costs down, there should be advantages in:

- spreading effective practice and avoiding replication of ideas and practice – reinventing the wheel should be much reduced!
- management systems across the numbers of schools involved should be able to be more efficient; and
- given the constant growth and development of online technology, communications across the collaborative structure should be easier and more economic.

Having said that, the funding for the group will need to be both adequate and appropriate and above all equitable. The issue of the lead school, if there is one, and how funding is allocated is a matter for debate. To give an example of what can enter that debate, consider the collaborative group that includes both deprived and affluent schools that reflect their specific localities. Schools in many countries have often been dedicated to raising funds (e.g. from parents) to purchase new equipment for 'their' school. Will this remain? Will collaborating schools be expected to share these extras or the additional income? How will parents view this?

Will there be sufficient leadership capacity?

On several occasions in this book, reference has been made to the need to increase leadership capacity, and various strategies have been mentioned as to how to achieve this. Particularly, the willingness and ability to offer shared leadership, opportunities for leadership experience, and appropriate training and development are all needed for success in this. Towards the end of the second decade of the twenty-first century, there remain serious concerns in both developed and developing countries about a relative shortfall in the numbers of people able and willing to apply for school leadership roles. It is, of course, another reason why the question about leaders not having to have been teachers is likely to be raised at various intervals! As populations age, and debates about retirement ages continue, no simple solutions seem available. Collaborative school leadership might appear superficial in offering a numerical aid in terms of the numbers required perhaps, but that is surely too facile an answer. Succession planning is crucial, and the opportunities for a planned approach to developing future leaders, we believe, is greatly enhanced by groups of schools working in collaboration. As Southworth (2007) argued, deputies and vice principals need the chance to work in several different schools to gain both experience and confidence to take on school leadership. The ideal opportunity is surely in these groups, and not merely at deputy level but in a range of leadership roles. Whereas secondments and job swapping across individual schools can be administratively cumbersome and potentially disruptive, as well as limiting in experience, the same is not true across schools in a collaborative group or chain, under the same governance, and with common approaches and values.

In the twenty-first century, it is possible that collaboration may become something that is seen as an entitlement – for schools, leaders and all those involved in and with schools. What was exceptional once may be seen as the norm. It will, of course, take different forms within the overall format of the educational system in particular countries. In developed countries with a large proportion of schools that have devolved responsibility and are semi-autonomous, collaboration will be the 'best choice'. In the United States for example, in an overall picture that Kolodny (2014: 150) describes as 'a cacophony of elaborate jigsaw pieces', collaboration is seen as one of the keys to the changes needed for improvement, while Mooyeri (2014: 130) sees collaboration as dismantling a reliance on hierarchical structures, leading to better decision making about learning in Canada. In England, the movement towards collaborative groupings in various forms is well advanced and is unlikely to be halted.

In countries with highly centralized educational systems, the impetus for collaboration will need to come from the centre providing resources and support, while in developing countries, the use of collaborative structures to reduce the isolation of schools and their leaders, notably in rural areas, will perhaps be recognized as the most effective way of raising overall standards to those of the best schools and thus providing support for this to happen.

What needs to be done

- Research should be ongoing into the various kinds of collaborative structures that exist – and new ones arising – to ascertain whether these may be ultimately the 'best choice'.
- Schools and collaborative groups should be increasingly autonomous with a view to develop the self-improving system envisaged by many.

- High accountability systems need to be developed as this autonomy develops – an accountability that is as minimal in bureaucracy as possible.
- New patterns of career paths, professional contracts and tenures should all be considered within the educational profession – many of these will reflect general trends in society at large, with more part-time leaders and flexibility over retirement ages.
- Training and development of collaborative school leaders will need to reflect the key elements of:
  - strategic thinking;
  - awareness of and commitment to sustainability;
  - enabling more emphasis on reflection and less on action;
  - the importance of positive professional relationships;
  - total commitment to social justice; and
  - commitment to the contribution that any school or group of schools can make to the wider educational system.

Whatever the context of such collaborative groupings, school leadership will remain one the key factors in school improvement and in raising attainment across educational systems. It will need to continue to develop, with those in leadership roles expanding their skills while retaining their individual characteristics. It will require a commitment from them to an understanding that the improvement of provision and opportunity for the children and young people in any one particular school is an integral and essential part of improving those things for all other children and young people, now and in the future. This deeply moral purpose has always existed in the very best educational and school leaders, but it will need to be more overtly stated and practised. Perhaps, effective collaborative school leadership can be a significant step towards improving educational opportunities for everyone.

References

Abaya, J. (2016). School leadership challenges along Kenya's Borabu-Sotik border. *EMAL, 44*(5), 757–774.

Abbott, I. (2004). Government initiatives: Excellence in cities and gifted and talented. In V. Brooks, I. Abbott, and P. Huddleston (eds), *Preparing to teach in the secondary school*. Maidenhead: Open University Press.

Abbott, I., Rathbone, M., and Whitehead, P. (2013). *Education policy*. London: Sage.

Ainscow, M. (2015). *Towards self-improving school systems: Lessons from a city challenge*. Abingdon: Routledge.

Armstrong, P. (2015). *Effective school partnerships and collaboration for school improvement: A review of the evidence*. London: DfE.

Arnold, R. (2006). *Schools in collaborations*. EMIE Report No 86. Slough: National Federation for Educational Research.

ASCL (2016a). *Staying in control of your school's destiny: Considering forming or joining a group of schools*. Leicester: ASCL.

ASCL (2016b). *Staying in control of your school's destiny: Joining a multi-academy trust*. Leicester: ASCL.

Baker, B., and Miron, G. (2013). *The business of charter schooling*. Boulder, CO: National Education Policy Centre.

Ball, S. (2003). Performance and fabrication in the education economy. In D. Gleeson and C. Husbands (eds), *The performing school*. London: Routledge.

Ball, S. (2012). The reluctant state and the beginning of the end of state education. *Journal of Educational Administration and History, 44*(2), 89–103.

Barnett, B., and O'Mahony, G. (2008). Mentoring and coaching programs for the professional development of school leaders. In J. Lumby, G. Crow, and P. Pashiardis (eds), *International handbook on preparation and development of school leaders*. London: Routledge.

Barrett-Baxendale, D., and Burton, D. (2009). Twenty first century headteacher: Pedagogue or visionary leader or both. *Journal of School Leadership and Management, 29*(2), 91–106.

Barrs, S., Bernardes, E., Elwick, A., Malartie, A., McInerney, I., Menzies, L., and Riggall, A. (2014). *Lessons from London: Investigating the success*. Reading: CfBT.

Beckett, F. (2007). *The great city academy fraud*. London: Continuum.

Begley, P. (ed.) (2009). *Values and educational leadership* (pp. 255–72). Albany: State University of New York Press.

Begley, P. (2010). Leading with moral purpose: The place of ethics. In T. Bush, L. Bell, and D. Middlewood (eds), *The principles of educational leadership and management*. London: Sage.

Bell, L. (1990). Ambiguity models of organisation: A case study of a comprehensive school. In T. Bush (ed.), *Management in education: Theory and practice* (pp 131–46). Milton Keynes: Open University Press.

Berwick, G., and Matthews, P. (2007). *The teaching school concept*. London: The London Leadership Strategy.

Bentley, T. (2002). Letting go: Complexity, individualism and the left. *Renewal, 10*(1, Winter).

Bentley, T., and Craig, J. (2006). *Presentation to NCSL advisory board.* London: DEMOS.

Bottery, M. (2004). *The challenges of educational leadership.* London: Paul Chapman.

Bottery, M. (2016). *Educational leadership for a more sustainable world.* London: Bloomsbury.

Boylan, M. (2016). Deepening system leadership: Teachers leading from below. *Educational Management Administration and Leadership, 44*(1), 57–72.

Brock, C. (2011). *Education as a global concern.* London: Continuum.

Brown, C. (2015). *Leading the use of research and evidence in schools.* London: IOE Press.

Burke, J. (2016). Getting to know the modern South Africa. *The Guardian,* August, p. 18.

Bush, T. (2003). *Theories of educational leadership and management* (3rd ed). London: Sage.

Bush, T. (2008). *Leadership development in education.* London: Sage.

Bush, T. (2016). Autonomy, accountability and moral purpose. *EMAL, 44*(5), 711–12.

Bush, T., and Middlewood, D. (2013). *Leading and managing people in education* (3rd ed). London: Sage.

Bush, T., Bell, L., and Middlewood, D. (2010). Introduction: New directions in educational leadership. In T. Bush, L. Bell, and D. Middlewood (eds), *The principles of educational leadership and management.* London: Sage.

Carpenter, D., and Peak, C. (2013). Leading charters: How charter administrators define their roles and their ability to lead. *Management in Education, 27*(4), 150–58.

Chapman, C. (2013). Academy federations, chains, and teaching schools in England: Reflections on leadership, policy and practice. *Journal of School Choice, 7,* 334–52.

Chapman, C. (2015). From one school to many: Reflections on the impact and nature of school federations and chains in England. *Educational Management Administration and Leadership, 43*(1), 46–60.

Chapman, C., and Muijs, D. (2014). Does school-to-school collaboration promote school improvement? A study of the impact of school federations on student outcomes. *School Effectiveness and School Improvement, 25*(3), 351–93.

Chapman, C., Muijs, D., and Collins, A. (2009). *The impact of federations on student outcomes.* Nottingham: National College for School Leadership.

Chapman, C., Muijs, D., and MacAllister, J. (2011). *A study of the impact of school federation on student outcomes.* Nottingham: National College Publications.

Chapman, C., Lindsay, G., Muijs, D., and Harris, A. (2010). The federations policy: From partnership to integration for school improvement? *School Effectiveness and Improvement, 21*(1), 53–74.

Chapman, J. (2002). *System failure.* London: DEMOS.

Chong, K., Stoll, K., and Low, G. (2003). Developing school leaders for a learning nation. In P. Hallinger (ed.), *Reshaping the landscape of school leadership development: A global perspective.* Lisse, The Netherlands: Swets and Zeitlings.

Cirin, R. (2014). *Do academies make use of their autonomy?* Research report. London: DfE.

Clarke, J., and Newman, J. (1997). *The managerial state: Power, politics and the ideology in the remaking of social welfare.* London: Sage.

Coldron, J., Crawford, M., Jones, S., and Simkins, T. (2014). The restructuring of schooling in England: The responses of well-positioned headteachers. *Educational Management, Administration and Leadership, 42*(3), 387–403.

Collarbone, P., and West-Burnham, J. (2008). *Understanding systems leadership: Securing equity and excellence in education*. London: Network Continuum.

Collins, A., Ireson, J., Stubbs, S., Nash, K., and Burnside, P. (2005). *New models of headship: Federations – Does every primary school need a headteacher? Key implications from a study of federations in The Netherlands*. Nottingham: National College for School Leadership.

Collins, J. (2006). *Good to great and the social sector*. London: Random House.

Collins, J., and Porras, J. (2011). *Built to last* (pp 201–202). New York: Harper Business Essentials.

Craig, J., and Bentley, T. (2005). *System leadership*. London: DEMOS/NCSL.

Cravens, X., Goldring, E., and Penaloza, R. (2012). Leadership practice in the context of US school choice reform. *Leadership and Policy in Schools*, *11*(4), 452–76.

Cuban, L. (1988). *The managerial imperative and the practice of leadership*. Albany, NY: State University of New York Press.

Day, C., and Schmidt, M. (2007). Sustaining resilience. In B. Davies (ed.), *Developing sustainable leadership*, London: Paul Chapman.

Day, C., Møller, J., Nusche, D. L., and Pont, B. (2008). The Flemish (Belgian) approach to system leadership. In B. Pont, D. Nusche, and D. Hopkins (eds), *Improving school leadership. Volume 2: Case studies on system leadership* (pp. 153–74). Paris: OECD.

Davies, B. (2006). *Leading the strategically focused school*. London: Paul Chapman.

Davies, B. (2007). Sustainable leadership. In B. Davies (ed.), Developing sustainable leadership. London: Paul Chapman.

DCSF. (2009). *Your child, your schools, our future: Building a 21st century schools system*. Cm 7588.

Desforges, C. (2006). *Collaboration for transformation: Why bother?* Nottingham: National College for School Leadership.

DfE. (2010). *The importance of teaching: A white paper*. London, DfE.

DfE. (2015). *School workforce census, 2015: Guide for school-employed staff*. London: DfE.

DfE. (2016). *Schools that work for everyone*. London: DfE.

DfE. (2016). Educational excellence everywhere. White paper. Retrieved 31 May 2016 from www.gov.uk/government/uploads/system/uploads/attachment_data/file/508447/Educational_Excellence_Everywhere.pdf

DfES. (2003). *Every child matters*. London: HMSO.

DfES. (2003). *National agreement on raising standards and tackling workload: A national agreement*. London: DfES.

DfES. (2004). *Five-year strategy for children and learners*. London: HMSO.

DfES. (2005). *Higher standards better schools for all. More choice for parents and pupils*. London: DfES.

Diamond, J., and Spillane, J. (2016). School leadership and management from a distributed perspective. *Management in Education*, *30*(4), 147–54.

Dryfoos, J., Quinn, J., and Barkin, C. (2005). *Community schools in action*. Oxford: Oxford University Press.

Dyson, A. (2006). What are we learning from research? In J. Piper (ed.), *Schools plus to extended schools*. Coventry: Continyou.

Farrell, C., Wohlstetter, P., and Smith, J. (2012). Charter management organizations: An emerging approach to scaling up what works. *Educational Policy*, *26*(4), 499–532.

Fellows, T (2016). *What makes a headteacher 'executive'? The role and responsibilities of executive headteachers in England*. National Governors Association.

Feys, E., and Devos, G. (2015). What comes out of incentivized collaboration: A qualitative analysis of eight Flemish networks. *EMAL*, *43*(5), 738–54.

Fink, D. (2005). *Leadership for mortals*. London: Paul Chapman.

Fox, J., and Evans, J. (2001). Leadership teams: All at sea. *Headship Matters*, 13, 3–4.

Frost, R. (2006). *Professionalism, partnerships and joined-up thinking*. Research in Practice 1. Dartington: Dartington Hall Trust.

Fullan, M. (1998). Leadership for the twenty first century: Breaking the bonds of dependency. *Educational Leadership*, *55*(7), 2–10.

Fullan, M. (2003). *The moral imperative of school leadership*. Thousand Oaks, CA: Corwin Press.

Fullan, M. (2004). *Systems thinkers in action: Moving beyond the standards plateau*. Nottingham: DfES.

Fullan, M. (2005). *Leadership and sustainability*. Thousand Oaks, CA: Corwin Press.

Fullan, M. (2006). *Turnaround leadership*. San Francisco, CA: Jossey-Bass.

Fullan, M., and Hargreaves, A. (1992). *What's worth fighting for in your school*. Buckingham: Open University Press.

Gee, J. (2002). New times and new literacies. In M. Kalantzis, G. Varnava-Skoura, and B. Cope (eds), *Learning for the future: New worlds, new literacies, new learning* (pp. 59–84). Melbourne: Common Round Publishing.

Gillinson, S., Hannon, C., and Gallagher, N. (2007). Learning together. In S. Parker and N. Gallagher (eds). *The collaborative state*. London: DEMOS.

Gold, A. (2010). Leading with values. In M. Coleman and D. Glover (eds), *Educational leadership and management: Developing insights and skills*. Maidenhead: Open University Press.

Goleman, D. (1996). *Working with emotional intelligence*. London: Bloomsbury.

Greany, T. (2014). *Are we nearly there yet? Progress, issues and possible next steps for a self-improving school system*. London: IOE Press.

Greany, T. (2015a). More fragmented, and yet more networked: Analysing the responses of two local authorities in England to the Coalition's 'self-improving school-led system' reforms. *London Review of Education*, *13*(2), 125–45.

Greany, T. (2015b). The self-improving school-led system in England: A review of evidence and thinking. *EMAL, 43*(2), 222–41.

Greany, T. (2016). *Innovation is possible: It's just not easy. Improvement, innovation and legitimacy in England's autonomous and accountable school system*. Leicester: ACSL.

Greenleaf, R. K. (1997). *Servant leadership*. New York: Paulist Press.

Gronn, P. (2010). Where to next for educational leadership? In T. Bush, L. Bell, and D. Middlewood (eds), *The principles of educational leadership and management* (pp. 70–86). London: Sage.

Gronn, P. (2016). Fit for purpose no more? *Management in Education*, *3*(4), 168–72.

Groundwater-Smith, S., and Mockler, N. (2003). *Learning to listen: Listening to learn*. University of Sydney.

Gu, Q., Rea, S., Smethem, L., Dunford, J., Varley, M., Sammons, P., Parish, N., Armstrong, P., and Powell, L. (2016). *Teaching schools evaluation: Final report*. London, DfE.

Gunter, H. M. (2012). *Leadership and the reform of education*. Briston: Policy Press.

Hall, D. (2013), Drawing a veil over managerialism: Leadership and the discursive disguise of the New Public Management. *Journal of Educational Administration and History*, *45*(3), 267–82.

Hall, V. (1999). Partnerships, alliances and competition: Defining the field. In J. Lumby and N. Foskett (eds), *Managing external relations in schools and colleges*. London, Paul Chapman.

Hall Jones, P. (2003). Managing a community primary school. In T. Gelsthorpe and J. West-Burnham (eds), *Educational leadership and the community*. London, Pearson Education.

Hamel, G., and Prahalad, C. (1996). *Competing for the future* (3rd ed.). New York: Harvard Business.

Hammersley-Fletcher, L. (2015). Values-driven decision-making: The ethics work of English headteachers within discourses of constraint. *EMAL*, *43*(22), 198–213.

Hanushek, E. Link, S., and Woessmann, L. (2012) Does school autonomy make sense everywhere? *Journal of Development Economics*, (104), 212–32.

Hargreaves, A. (2010). Change from without: Lessons from other countries, systems, and sectors. In A. Hargreaves, A. Lieberman, M. Fullan, and D. Hopkins (eds), *Second international handbook of educational change*. New York: Springer.

Hargreaves, A., and Fink, D. (2005). *Sustaining leadership*. San Franscisco: Jossey-Bass.

Hargreaves, A., and Fullan, M. (2012). *Professional capital*. Abingdon, Routledge.

Hargreaves, A., Halász, G. and Beatriz, P. (2008). The Finnish approach to system leadership. In B. Pont, D. Nusche and D. Hopkins, *Improving school leadership. Volume 2: Case studies on system leadership*. Paris: OECD.

Hargreaves, D. (2011). *Leading a self-improving school system*. Nottingham: National College for School Leadership.

Hargreaves, D. (2012). *A self-improving school system: Towards maturity*. Nottingham: National College for School Leadership.

Hargreaves, D. (2014). A self-improving school system and its potential for reducing inequality. *Oxford Review of Education*, *40*(6), 696–714.

Hargreaves, D. H. (2003). *Education epidemic: Transforming secondary schools through innovation networks*. London: DEMOS.

Hargreaves, D. H. (2010). *Creating a self-improving school system*. Nottingham: National College for Leadership of Schools and Children's Services.

Harris, A. (2005). Foreword. In D. Fink (ed.), *Leadership for mortals*. London: Paul Chapman.

Harris, A. (2009). *Distributed leadership: Different perspectives*. The Netherlands: Springer.

Harris, A. (2013). Distributed leadership: Friend or foe? *Educational Management Administration & Leadership*, *41*(5), 545–54.

Harris, A., Brown, D., and Abbott, I. (2006). Executive leadership: Another lever in the system? *School Leadership and Management*, *26*(4), 397–409.

Hatcher, R. (2005). The distribution of leadership and power in schools. *British Journal of Sociology of Education*, *26*(2), 253–67.

Hatcher, R. (2008). System leadership, networks and the question of power. *Management in Education*, *22*(2), 24–30.

Hays, P. (2013). Narrowing the gap: Three key dimensions of site-based leadership in four Boston charter public schools. *Education and Urban Society*, *45*(1), 37–87.

Heifetz, R. A. (1994). *Leadership without easy answers*. Harvard, MA: Belknap Press.

Hill, R. (2010). *Chain reactions: A thinkpiece on the development of chains of schools in the English school system*. Nottingham, National College for Leadership of Schools and Children's Services.

Hill, R. (2011). *The importance of teaching and the role of system leadership: A commentary on the Illuminas research for the National College*. Nottingham: National College for School Leadership.

Hill, R., and Mathews, P. (2008). *School leading schools: The power and potential of National Leaders of Education*. Nottingham: National College for School Leadership.

Hill, R., Dunford, J., Parish, N., Rea, S., and Sandals, L. (2012). *The growth of academy chains: implications for leaders and leadership*. Nottingham: National College for School Leadership.

Higham, R. (2010). Federations and system leadership. In A. Hargreaves, A. Lieberman, M. Fullan and D. Hopkins (eds), *Second international handbook of educational change* (pp. 725–39). New York: Springer.

Higham, R., Hopkins, D., and Matthews, P. (2009). *System leadership in practice*. London: Routledge Falmer.

Hiron, G., and Nelson, C. (2002). *What's public about charter schools? Lessons learned about choice and accountability*. Thousand Oaks, CA: Corwin Press.

Hopkins, D. (2006). A short primer on system leadership. Paper presented at the Conference of International Perspectives on School Leadership for Systemic Improvement. 6 July, OECD.

Hopkins, D., and Higham, R. (2007). System leadership: Mapping the landscape. *School Leadership and Management*, *27*(2), 147–66.

Hodgson, P. (1987). Managers can be taught but leaders have to learn. *ICT*, November/December, 14–23.

Hummerstone, C. (2012). *Leadership skills and behaviours of executive head teachers*. Nottingham: National College of Teaching and Leadership.

Hutchings, M., Greenwood, C., Hollingsworth, S., Mansoray, A., and Rose, A. (2012). *Evaluation of the city challenge programme*. London: DoE.

Jensen, B., and Clark, A. (2013). *Confident school leadership: An East Asian perspective*. Nottingham: National College for Teaching and Leadership.

Kerr, K., and West, M. (eds) (2010). *Insight 2: Social inequality: Can schools narrow the gap? A review of the evidence for the British Educational Research Association*. London: British Educational Research Association.

Kofman, F., and Senge, P.M. (1995). Communities of commitment: The heart of learning organizations. In S. Chawla and J. Renesch (Eds), *Learning irganizations: Developing cultures for tomorrow'sworkplace*. Oregon: Productivity Press.

Kolodny, K. (2014). Contemporary schooling in the United States: An overview. In D. E. Mulcahy, D. G. Mulcahy, and R. Saul (eds), *Education in North America* (pp. 138–153). London: Bloomsbury.

Lake, R., Dusseault, B., Bowen, M., Demeritt, A., and Hill, P. (2010). *The national study of Charter Management Organization (CMO) effectiveness: Report on interim findings*. Center on Reinventing Public Education, University of Washington.

Le Grand, J., and Bartlett, W. (1993). *Quasi-markets and social policy*. Basingstoke: MacMillan.

Leithwood, K., Day, C., Sammons, P., Harris, A., and Hopkins, D. (2006). *Seven strong claims about successful school leadership*. Nottingham: NCSL and DfES.

Levin, B. (2012). *System-wide improvement in education*. UNESCO and The International Academy of Education.

Lindsay, G., Mujis, D., Harris, A., Chapman, C., Arweck, E., and Goodall, J. (2007). *Schools federation pilot study, 2003–2007*. London: DCSF.

Lord, P., Wespieser, K., Harland, J., Fellows, T., and Theobald, K. (2016). *Executive headteachers: What's in a name? A full report of the findings*. Slough, Birmingham and London: NFER, NGA and TFLT.

Lumby, J. (1999). Achieving responsiveness. In J. Lumby and N. Foskett (eds), *Managing external relations in schools and colleges*. London: Paul Chapman.

Lumby, J. (2016). Distributed leadership as fashion or fad. *Management in Education*, *30*(4), 164–167.

Lumby, J., Crow, G., and Pashiardos, P. (2008). Epilogue. In J. Lumby, G. Crow, and P. Pashiardos (eds), *International handbook of preparation and development of school leaders*. London: Routledge.

March, J., and Olsen, J. (1989). *Rediscovering institutions: The organizational basis of politics*. New York: Free Press.

Matthews, P., and Berwick, G. (2013). *Teaching schools: First among equals?* Nottingham: National College for Teaching and Leadership.

Matthews, P., and Hill, R. (2010). Improving schools through collaboration: A mixed methods study of school-to-school partnerships in the primary sector. *Oxford Review of Education, 41*(5), 562–86.

Matthews, P., Rea, S., Hill, R., and Gu, Q. (2014). *Freedom to lead: A study of outstanding primary school leadership in England*. Research report. ISOS. Retrieved 19 May 2016 from www.gov.uk/government/publications

McLaughlin, K., Osborn, S., and Ferlie, E. (2002). *New Public Management: Current trends and future prospects*. London: Routledge.

Mestry, R. (2014). A critical analysis of national norms and standards of school funding policy in South Africa. *EMAL, 42*(6), 851–67.

Middlewood, D. (1998). Strategic management: An overview. In D. Middlewood and J. Lumby (eds), *Strategic management in schools and colleges*. London: Paul Chapman.

Middlewood, D. (2013). Why is school leadership unique? In R. Parker, with D. Middlewood (eds), *The reality of school leadership*. London: Bloomsbury.

Middlewood, D., and Abbott, I. (2015). *Improving professional learning through in-house inquiry*. London: Bloomsbury.

Middlewood, D., and Abbott, I. (2017a). *Managing staff for improved performance: Human resource management for schools*. London: Bloomsbury.

Middlewood, D., and Abbott, I. (2017b). Developing a culture for sustainability in educational organisations. In R. Papa and A. Saiti (eds), *Building for a sustainable future in our schools: brick by brick*. Switzerland: Springer.

Middlewood, D., and Parker, R. (2009). *Leading and managing extended schools*. London: Paul Chapman.

Middlewood, D., Parker, R., and Beere, J. (2005). *Creating a learning school*. London: Paul Chapman.

Middlewood, D., Abbott, I., Netshandema, V., and Whitehead, P. (2017). Collaborative school leadership: The more heads the better. In P. Miller (ed.), *Cultures of educational leadership: Global and international responses*. London: Springer.

Miller, P. (2017). Researching and theorising common issues in different world contexts. In P. Miller (ed.), Cultures of educational leadership. London: Palgrave MacMillan.

Mintzberg, H. (1995). Strategic thinking as seeing. In B. Garrett (ed.), *Developing strategic thought*. London: HarperCollins.

Mintzberg, H. (2004). *Managers not MBAs: A hard look at the soft practice of manging and management development*. San Franscisco: Berrett-Koehler.

Moayeri, M. (2014). Moving towards a more independent and collaborative culture. In D.E. Mulcahy, D.G. Mulcahy, and R. Saul (eds), *Education in North America*. London: Bloomsbury.

Morris, E. (2001). Professionalism and trust – The future of teachers and teaching. A speech by the Secretary of State for Education to the social market foundation. 12 November. London: SMF.

Mortimore, P. (2013). *Education under siege*. Bristol: Policy Press.

Mourshed, M., Chijioke, C., and Barber, M. (2010). *How the world's most improved school systems keep getting better*. London: McKinsey and Co.

Muijs, D. (2015). Improving schools through collaboration: A mixed methods study of school-to-school partnerships in the primary sector. *Oxford Review of Education*, *41*(5), 563–86.

Muijs, D., West, M., and Ainscow, M. (2010). Why network? Theoretical perspectives on networking and collaboration between schools. *School Effectiveness and School Improvement*, 21, 5–26.

National College for Leadership of Schools and Children's Services. (2010). *Executive heads. Summary report*. Nottingham: National College for Leadership of Schools and Children's Services.

National College for School Leadership. (2007). *Leadership succession: An overview*. Nottingham: NCSL.

National School Board Association. (n.d.) *What is systemic change?* Retrieved from www.nsba.org/sbot/toolkit/whatsc.html

NCTL. (2013a). *System leadership: Supported schools impact analysis*. Nottingham: NCTL.

NCTL. (2013b). *School leadership for a self-improving system*. Seminar, 27–28 November. Nottingham: NCTL.

NCTL. (2014). *The governance of federations*. Nottingham: NCTL.

NCTL. (2015a). *Teaching schools: The school perspective*. Nottingham: NCTL.

NCTL. (2015b). *Business plan 1 April 2015–31 March 2016*. Retrieved 25 April 2016 from www.gov.uk/government/uploads/system/uploads/attachment_data/file/416941/nctl-business-plan-2015-to-16.pdf

OECD. (2015). *Schooling redesigned: Towards innovative learning systems: The school perspective*. Paris: OECD.

Ofsted. (2005). *Independent/state school partnerships*. HMI 2305. London: Ofsted.

Ozga, J. (1995). Deskilling professionals: Professionalization, deprofessionalisation and managerialism. In H. Busher and R. Saran (eds), *Managing teachers as professional in schools*. London: KoganPage.

Paino, W., Renzulli, L., Boylan, R., and Bradley, C. (2014). For grades or money? Charter school failure in North Carolina, *Educational Administration Quarterly*, *50*(3), 501–36.

Papa, R., and Saiti, A. (2016). *Building for a sustainable future in education: Brick by brick*. New York: Springer.

Parker, R. with Middlewood, D. (2013). *The reality of school leadership*. London: Bloomsbury.

Pepper, C. (2014). Leading for sustainability in Western Australian regional schools. *EMAL*, *42*(4), 506–19.

Peters, T. (2003). *Re-imagine! Business excellence in a disruptive age*. New York: DK Publishing.

Piot, L., and Kelchtermans, G. (2016). The micorpolics of distributed leadership: Four case studies of school federations. *Educational Management Administration Leadership*, *44*(4), 632–49.

Policy Exchange. (2009). *A guide to school choice reforms*. London: Policy Exchange.

Pont, B., and Hopkins, D. (2008a). Approaches to system leadership: Lessons learned and policy pointers. In Pont, B., Nusche, D., and Hopkins, D. (eds), *Improving school leadership. Volume 2: Case studies on system leadership* (pp. 253–71). Paris: OECD.

Pont, B., Nusche, D., and Moorman, H. (2008b) *Improving school leadership. Volume 1: Policy and practice*. Paris: OECD.

Preedy, M. (1999). Collaboration between schools. In J. Lumby and N. Foskett (eds), *Managing external relations in schools and colleges*. London: Paul Chapman.

Prew, M. (2009). Modifying school improvement concepts to the needs of South African township schools. *EMAL*, *37*(6), 824–46.

Rifkin, J. (2004). *The European dream: How Europe's future is quietly eclipsing the American dream*. New York: Tarcher/Penguin.

Riley, K., and MacBeath, J. (2003). Effective leaders and effective schools. In N. Bennett, M. Crawford, and M. Cartwright (eds), *Effective educational leadership* (pp. 173–85). London: Paul Chapman.

Robinson, S. (2011). Primary headteachers: New leadership roles inside and outside the school. *Educational Management Administration Leadership*, *37*(3), 378–408.

Robinson, S. (2012). *School and system leadership*. London: Continuum.

Salokangas, M., and Chapman, C. (2014). Exploring governance in two chains of academy schools: A comparative case study. *Educational Management Administration Leadership*, *42*(3), 372–86.

Santane, S. (2017). Beyond neoliberalism: Education for sustainable development and a new paradigm of global cooperation. In R. Papa and A. Saiti (eds), *Building for a sustainable future in our schools: Brick by brick*. Switzerland: Springer.

Search Institute. (2000). *Asset building*. Retrieved from www.search-institute.org

Sendl, L. (2007). Mentoring – A new mantra for education? *Teaching and Teacher Education*, *55*(2), 246–78.

Senge, P. (1990). *The fifth discipline: The art and practice of the learning organisation*. London: Random House.

Simkins, T., Coldron, J., Jones, S. and Crawford, M. (2015). System leaders in local landscapes in England. Paper presented at ECER 2015, Budapest.

Slater, L. (2008). Pathways to building leadership capacity. *EMAL*, *36*(1), 55–69.

Smith, E. (2015). What happened to the Beacon Schools? Policy reform and equity. *Oxford Review of Education*, *41*(3), 367–86.

Southworth, G. (2007). Leadership succession. In B. Davies (ed.), *Developing sustainable leadership*. London: Paul Chapman.

Southworth, G. (2008). Primary school leadership today and tomorrow. *School Leadership and Management*, *28*(5), 413–34.

Spillane, J., Diamond, B., Sherer, J., and Coldren, A. (2005). Distributing leadership. In M. Coles and G. Southworth (eds), *Developing leadership creating the schools of tomorrow*. London: Oxford University Press.

Spring, J. (2008). Research on globalization and education. *Review of Educational Research*, *78*(2), 330–63.

Stevenson, H. (2007). Improvement through collaboration and competition – Can the government have it both ways? *Management in Education*, *21*(1), 29–33.

Timperley, H., and Robinson, V. (1998). The micropolitics of accountability. *Educational Policy*, *12*(2), 162–76.

Todd, L. (2007). *Partnerships for inclusive education*. Abingdon: Routledge.

Townsend, T. (2012). School leadership in the twenty-first century: Different approaches to common problems? *School Leadership and Management*, *31*(2), 93–103.

Tugade, M., Frederickson, B., and Feldman Barrett, L. (2004). Psychological resilience and positive emotion granularity: Examining the benefits of positive emotions on coping and health. *Journal of Personality*, *72*(6), 1162–90.

Welbourn, D., Warwick, R., Carnall, C., and Fathers, D. (2012). *Leadership of whole systems*. Retrieved 30 March 2016 from www.kingsfund.org.uk/sites/files/kf/leadership-whole-systems-welbourn-warwick-carnall-fathers-leadership-review2012-paper.pdf

West-Burnham, J. (2000). Education, leadership and the community. In T. Gelsthorpe and J. West-Burnham (eds), *Educational leadership and the community*. London: Pearson Education.

West-Burnham, J. (2006). Extended schools 2020: Prospects and possibilities. In J. Piper (ed.), *From schools plus to extended schools*. Coventry: Continyou.

West-Burnham, J. (2011). *Building sustainable school improvement through systems leadership and collaboration*. Nottingham: National College for School Leadership.

Williams, P. (2002). The competent boundary spanner. *Public Administration*, 8(1).

Wilshaw, M. (2016). *Focused inspections of academies in multi-academy trusts. Letter to the Secretary of State*. London: Ofsted.

Wood, M. (2002). *The demise of the superhead*. London: Optimus.

Woods, P., and Simkins, T. (2014). Understanding the local: Themes and issues in the experience of structural reform in England. *Educational Management Administration and Leadership*, *42*(3), 324–40.

Yuen, J., Chen, D., and Ng, D. (2016). Distributed leadership through the lens of activity theory, *EMAL*, *44*(5), 814–36.

Index